A Little
JOY

A Little
OY

Other Andrews McMeel Publishing Books by
Marnie Winston-Macauley

He Says/She Says

ManSpeak:
What He Says . . . What He Really Means

Men We Love to Hate:
The Book

The Ultimate
Answering Machine Message Book

The Ultimate
Sex, Love & Romance Quiz Book 1

The Ultimate
Sex, Love & Romance Quiz Book 2

A Little
JOY

A Little
OY

JEWISH WIT AND WISDOM

MARNIE WINSTON-MACAULEY

**Andrews McMeel
Publishing**

Kansas City

Prepared with the assistance of Simon Louis Winston-Macauley

01 02 03 04 05 BIN 10 9 8 7 6 5 4 3 2 1

ISBN: 0-7407-1867-3

Library of Congress Catalog Card Number: 2001086431

Dedication

To the memory of those who taught me Yiddishkeit,
*Shirley and Louis Winston, and for those
who preceded them*

To the long and happy life of Yiddishkeit *for my son,
Simon, and for my nephew, Justus, and for those
who shall follow them*

Contents

Preface

December 1993. The scene: Riverdale, New York, an almost entirely Jewish enclave directly north of Manhattan. I am wearing a gold lamé strapless I picked up at an upscale resale shop, reduced from $2,000 to $150, that no doubt was originally "gently" worn by a bulimic heiress. True, the waist was around my neck, however at that price I would have worn a kitchen curtain.

I digress.

My boss at the time, the late, ever fascinating, Douglas Marland, head writer of the daytime drama *As the World Turns,* is picking me up for an evening of theater.

As I tumble into the car, he looks at me oddly. Okay, yes, the dress frightened him. (He was terrified I would show up next to him at the Emmys looking like an aging neon hooker.) But more to the point . . .

Here we are, a few days before Christmas. Houses in every hamlet across America are strung with red and green lights—and then there is here. A tiny turf in the Bronx with nothing but the faint orange glow of Menorahs peeking out of windows demurely into the winter night.

"Where the heck are we?" he asks, awestruck. "Tel Aviv?"

Undaunted, I explain. Which kicks off a discussion of what it was like to grow up in the fifties as a Jew—in a non-Jewish neighborhood, which I did as a kid.

Brilliant, verbal, and glib, this master storyteller is rendered speechless.

Finally . . . "You know, it never once occurred to me what it must feel like to be an outsider on Christmas." And he remained pensive for the rest of the evening.

He got it. You see, he, too, was an outsider. A farm boy who spent every waking moment he could at the movies—dreaming.

In that instant, we both finally understood that silent bond we had always shared.

> The Jews are like other people, only more so.
>
> —PROVERB

August 1961: The scene: London, England. The author is twelve years old and traveling with the family. Dad is driving. Actually, he is swerving, hopelessly lost somewhere in the East End. When our Rover careens into a pushcart, he finally decides to *ask*. Getting out of the car, Dad approaches the proprietor of the cart, and they briefly shake hands.

After resorting to miming, because the Cockney is incomprehensible to us, Dad impulsively utters the sigh: "oy."

The man suddenly stops with the "blimeys" and, bursting with excitement, shouts, "*Farshtaist* [understand] *Yiddish?*"

To which Dad replies, "*Nu, vo den?* [So, what else?]"

And the two men shake hands again, this time with palpable warmth. As though they are meeting anew. Two *lantsmen*—countrymen—who lived thousands of miles apart, who had never met, and who never would again. Yet there was an undeniable connection.

A shared bond.

And with that one handshake, I, at the age of twelve, instantly understood. A feeling that took five thousand years to evolve. A feeling that even fifty thousand words can't evoke quite as well, half as poignantly—but I hope these will help.

Acknowledgments

Finding just the right balance between the "joys" and the "oys" was a magnificent task—and an overwhelming one. Over two hundred and fifty sources were used, and even they were but a nick (okay, a decent scratch) beneath the surface. But one does not accomplish this kind of research by books or even the Internet alone. It takes people. Special people of great devotion, unerring patience, and endurance (not to mention guilt and payoffs).

For their generosity in allowing me to pick their brains, their humor, and part of their lives: the legends, brilliant all. In alphabetical order, Bernie Allen, Marty Allen, Sir Arthur C. Clarke, Pat Cooper, Pudgy! and Mike Cardella (her husband, creative director), Sandy Hackett, Jay Leno, Freddie Roman, and Stan Zimmerman. I add to this a bright, talented, comic newcomer, Dale Mathias.

Verify, verify, verify! This is the motto of any good nonfiction writer or reporter. As you shall see, some of the information herein is different, stimulating, enlightening, and, yes, weird. Or hard to get. To help me go that extra furlong, Michael McDonough, at Music Theatre International (MTI); Professor Tony Rothman, Illinois Wesleyan University; the Oklahoma Historical Society;

Temple Emanu-El; Congregation Shearith Israel; *Moment* magazine, Levi Strauss & Co., the B. Manischewitz Company—and, of course, Broadway's Jerusalem II (The Flying Pizza People!).

And then there are my editors. Bless every one of them: Jennifer Fox, Michael Nonbello, and Kris Melcher. When we started this project, some may have thought "oy" was . . . maybe a little Scottish, out there in Kansas City, Missouri. Well, this talented, ambitious group rose to the cultural challenge, once again proving what *mensches* they are. And for getting it off the bookshelves and into your hands, the credit goes to Kristine Abbott, director of publicity, and Deborah Broide, our guardian angel in New York.

On a personal note, to my Aunt Norma Greisman, the family matriarch, who, a mere stripling in her mid-nineties, helped her ignorant niece wade through the Yiddish. Also much gratitude to the Jerusalem-born Elana Silberstein, Nevada realtor extraordinaire, who is a fountain of Jewish and Israeli humor—and graciously shared it. Were it not for the computer genius of Dmitry Lev, Elevated Computing (Las Vegas), half of this manuscript (which crashed) might still be in the ether.

And, to the loves of my life—who helped save mine on this huge project. My husband, Ian, a brilliant editor, who actually didn't fight with me too much and let me be "the boss of him" (swear, no Monica jokes). And especially to my assistant, the only one who knows what a cache file is and how to get rid of one, our son, Simon Louis Winston-Macauley. His research, his humor, his conceptual and intellectual judgment were faultless. Not only did he help create and validate the work but he gave his mother a little *nakhes* (pride)—even though, alas, *he* didn't let me be "the boss of him."

I know what one must do to be Jewish. He must assume his Jewishness. He must assume his collective conscience. He must assume his past with its sorrows and its joys.
—ELIE WIESEL

[The trick is in finding the right balance between transmitting] the oys and joys of Jewish life.
—DEBORAH E. LIPSTADT
(contemporary U.S. historian, author)

Introduction

This is not a reference book about everything Jewish. It is not a dictionary, an encyclopedia, a catalog, a chronology, a ranking, a thesaurus, a guide, an almanac, a list, a compendium—or any other literary term like "complete" (or compleat) that implies or bestows *mavinhood* (expertise) upon the reader (or, for that matter, the writer) about Judaica. It is not a joke book, a cookbook, a history book, biographies, or a triviata. It is not written for Jewish scholars, or serious students of Jewish culture (although they can enjoy it). It is not a studious appraisal. Entries are not democratic, nor are they complete. To be sure, they were checked and rechecked thoroughly and carefully. Over 250 sources were used, as the source list at the end indicates, to ensure that the most accurate information has been provided. Where there were differences of fact, the predominant opinion was used. When doubts persisted, the entry was deleted. Final choices, however, were made by the author, solely on the basis of personal editorial judgment, and limited by page count constraints. The Yiddish transliterations were based on several published sources.

WHAT THIS BOOK IS

This is a book that reflects a feeling, for at least this author, of being Jewish today. It illustrates the majesty, diversity, the vitality of a culture whose richness pervades all aspects of life. The chapters reflect that variety, from humor to foods, language, history, and pathos. More than a *bisel* (little) this or that, themes are written somewhat "musically." Choices of material, particularly those reflecting the joys and oys, were selected from the heart to reach the heart of the reader—whether through remembrance or through introduction. To share and experience an essence of *Yiddishkeit* beyond the words. In reading, I hope you'll hear the rhythms.

The J(Oys) of Jewish Humor

J ewish humor is universal. Most people "get it," or Jackie Mason would be playing Brighton Beach instead of Broadway and *Seinfeld* would be a summer replacement on cable 99 in Century Village instead of a megahit from Canarsie to the cornfields. And what they're "getting" in those fields and on the Strip ain't pastrami on white.

OY, DON'T ASK!

Yes, after much debate and research on Jewish humor, I came up with something surprising.

Suffering is involved. (All right, you may *klop* (slap) me—*make it with corned beef.*) The late Steve Allen (who was not Jewish) estimated that about 80 percent of America's leading humorists over the past forty years have been Jewish, saying,

> To me, the Jews are funnier . . . than any other group. Why? Because they have had more trouble. And trouble is often the heart of humor. . . . Traditional Jewish humor often converts a joke into a form of social comment or criticism. It must not be supposed . . . that . . . [it] is only a weapon with which they subtly strike back at a bullying world. A great

1

deal of their laughter is directed at themselves. Self-criticism is one of the earmarks of Jewish comedy.

Yes, like a good *tsibeleh* (onion) we Jews are a complex pastiche, layered with strands of oys running through the joys. Perhaps my favorite comment on this intimate relationship between Jewish humor and pain was made by the comedy writer and producer Larry Gelbart, who said, "A Jewish male, who starts life by receiving the unkindest cut of all, expects the worst from then on and is rarely disappointed. . . . He will find a cloud in every silver lining. He will tell you to have a nice day, knowing with all his heart that that's impossible. . . . Jews. It's not that it only hurts when we laugh—we only laugh when we hurt. And that's pretty much all the time." (True, this wouldn't explain an Elayne Boosler or Rita Rudner—but, as with "all men are created equal," we can extrapolate.)

Now, I can bore us senseless with kakababble about why we make a joke when Cossacks are chasing us (okay, after)—but you know all that.

So, how have we survived? With a little help from our . . .

Yiddisher Kops (Jewish Heads)

A cruise ship sinks and Johnson, a Christian; Ahmad, a Muslim; and Kornfeld, a Jew, make it to an uninhabited island.

Johnson tears branches from a palm tree, creates a cross, and prays to be rescued.

Ahmad pulls fronds from the palm tree, creates a mat, and prays to Allah to save him.

Kornfeld falls asleep under the palm tree.

"How could he be so calm in such a disaster?" the other two ask.

Kornfeld opens an eye. "I pledged three million to the Jewish Federation. Don't worry. They'll find me."

Just as the army marches on its stomach, so have Jews marched on and survived the millennia with a little help from our humor and one of the grandest of survival tools, our *Yiddisher kops*—our Jewish brains and wit.

· · · ● · · ·

Three men are about to be executed and are asked what they wish for their last meal.

Carlucci asks for a pepperoni pizza—which he is served. And then he's executed.

La Pierre requests filet mignon—which he is served. And then he's executed.

Finkel asks for a plate of fresh strawberries.

"Strawberries?" says the warden. "But they're out of season!"

"So nu," says Finkel, "I'll wait."

Airman Cohen was assigned to advise new recruits about G.I. insurance. Captain Smith noticed he had almost 100 percent sales. So the captain stood in the back of the room and listened to Cohen's pitch. Cohen explained the basics, then added: "If you have G.I. insurance and go into battle and are killed, the government pays $200,000 to your beneficiaries. If you don't have G.I. insurance and you go into battle and get killed, the government only has to pay $6,000.

"So, you tell me," he concluded, "who are they going to send into battle first?"

• • ● • • •

A medieval Jewish astrologer told a king his mistress would soon die. She did, *nebech* (pity). The outraged king, sure it was the astrologer's prophecy that killed her, summoned him.

"Prophesy to me when *you* shall die!" commanded the angry king.

Oy vay, thought the astrologer, realizing the king would kill him immediately no matter what his answer. "I have no date, sire," he said, thinking fast. "However, according to the charts . . . whenever I die, Your Highness shall die three days later."

Did you ever see anybody afraid to walk into a Jewish neighborhood because he might get killed by an accountant?

—JACKIE MASON

Quiz: What won't you ever hear in a Jewish home?

Answer: "Darling, put down the book and go give that bad boy a *klop* (punch)."

As you may have noticed, *Yiddisher kops* don't generally involve protective cups. Jews hold many things dear, but fighting isn't one of them, as we believe in survival by intellect over violence (except when it involves the Israeli Army).

Two Classics

Goldfarb and Bronstein are walking in a tough neighborhood when they spot two burly locals coming toward them.

"Uh-oh," says Goldfarb. "We better make a run for it. There are two of them, and only one of us."

• • • ● • • •

Eventually, the two are facing a firing squad. All the rifles are trained on them when the guard asks if they have one last request.

"I wouldn't mind a cigarette," says Bronstein.

"Sha," whispers Goldfarb. "Don't make trouble."

No. A most important aspect of the *Yiddisher kop* isn't fisticuffs—it is logic.

But on the Other Hand:
Not-So-Simple Logic

You may have noticed that a most important aspect of the *Yiddisher kop* is logic. Whether penetrating examination, startling conclusion, hysterical irony, or sheer absurdity, the Jewish psyche loves logic even more than lox (with a shmear).

A Classic

Goldstein is returning by train to his home, a small town, and talks with a young stranger, Levine, also heading there.

"You're on business?" Goldstein asks.

"No. It's social."

"You have relatives there?"

"No."

"Married?"

"No."

Goldstein thinks: Not married, not business, no relatives . . . so why is he going? To meet a girl—her family. Such a shlep means an engagement! But to whom? There are three other Jewish families. . . . The Resnicks? No, sons only. The Feldsteins? The daughter's married. The Cohens? Hmmm . . . Hannah's always with books. . . . Aha! It must be Rachel!

"Mazel Tov on your forthcoming marriage to Rachel Cohen!" says Goldstein.

"But . . . we've told no one! How did you know?" stutters the young man, aghast.

"Obvious." Goldstein smiles.

. . . ● . . .

Every stick has two ends

—JEWISH PROVERB

. . . ● . . .

Mrs. Goldfarb is wheeling her grandson in a baby carriage. A woman stops her.

"What a beautiful baby," she says.

"Ah, this is nothing! You should see his pictures!"

• • • ● • • •

A Miami officer pulls over eighty-six-year-old Mrs. Posner because her signals were confusing.

"First you put your hand up, like you're turning left, then you wave your hand up and down, then you turn right," says the officer.

"I decided not to turn left," she explains.

"Then why the up and down?"

"Officer." She sniffs. "I was erasing!"

• • • ● • • •

Abe's son arrives home from school puffing and panting. "Dad, you'll be so proud of me. I saved a dollar by running behind the bus all the way home!"

"Big deal!" said Abe. "You could have run behind a taxi and saved twenty!"

• • • ● • • •

Yankel is twenty-five and has never had a date. When the Rabbi tells him it's time already, Yankel explains he can't talk to girls.

"Talk about her family, what she likes. And if that fails, talk philosophy," says the Rabbi.

For days Yankel repeats, "Family . . . likes . . . philosophy." "Family . . . likes . . . philosophy." So armed, he goes out with Rachel. The two sit silently in the deli.

"So," Yankel blurts, "do you have any brothers?"

"No," says Rachel.

Silence.

"Do you like baseball?"

"No."

At a loss, Yankel recalls, Philosophy! In his best Talmudic tones, he leans forward and asks, "So nu, if you *had* a brother, *would* he like baseball?"

• • • ◉ • •

Goldberg was retiring and turning the business over to his son.

"My boy," he said, "I have succeeded in business because of two principles: honesty and wisdom. Honesty means, if you promise a shipment on the twenty-second of March, come H—— or high water, you deliver."

"And wisdom?" asked the son.

"Dope! Who asked you to promise?"

How does Goldberg know? Because Jews are *mavins* (experts).

Mavinhood

There is scarcely a situation (except maybe how to pick out a lug nut) about which we are not experts. Even when we're not.

Two Classics

Morris and Izzy are sitting over corned beef discussing the meaning of the cosmos.

"Life," says Morris, "is like a bowl of tuna fish."

Izzy is quiet, considering. "So, why is life like a bowl of tuna fish?" he asks finally.

"How should I know? What am I, a philosopher?"

• • • ● • • •

Finkel brings very fine material to Mendel the tailor and asks him to make a pair of pants. Week after week the pants aren't ready. Finally, after six weeks they're done. And they're a perfect fit!

"You know," he says. "It took G-d only six days to make the world. And here, it took you six weeks to make one pair of pants."

"Ah," says Mendel. "But look at this pair of pants—and look at the world!"

• • • ● • • •

"Three Jews, Three Opinions" (Yiddish Proverb)

Not only are Jews experts about most things—
rarely will the experts agree.

· · · ● ● · · ·

Four Rabbis engage in theological arguments, and it's always three against one.

Finally, the odd Rabbi out appeals to a
higher authority. "G-d!" he cries. "I know I am
right! Please, a sign to prove it to them!"

Suddenly, from a sunny day, it pours.

"A sign from G-d! See, I'm right!"

The other three disagree, saying storms
often cool hot days.

So again: "Please, G-d, a bigger sign!"

Lightning slams a tree.

"Is that not a sign from G-d!" cries the Rabbi.

"A sign of nature!" they insist, again making
it three to one.

Just as the Rabbi is about to beg an even
bigger sign, the sky blackens and a voice
intones, "HEEEEEEEE'S RIIIIIIIGHT!"

The Rabbi, hands on hips, says, "Well . . . ?"

The others shrug. "So now it's three to two."

· · · ● ● · · ·

A Rabbi in the hospital received a large vase
of flowers with the following note:

"The congregation wishes you a speedy and
complete recovery—by a vote of 212 to 74!"

A forestry graduate is given his first post in a huge forest in the middle of nowhere. In his survival gear he finds a recipe for matzah balls. Confused, he asks his superior, Goldberg, about it.

"In a few years, when you've had it already with the bears and trees and you're going a little *meshugge* (nuts) from the silence and the solitude, you'll remember your matzah ball recipe. And, when you do, get it out and start making some," says Goldberg.

"And what will that do?" asks the graduate.

"Before you know it, you'll have ten Jewish women looking over your shoulder, shouting, "You think that's the right way to make a matzah ball?'"

A Classic

The president of the United States is meeting with the president of Israel.

"The problem of leadership is sometimes overwhelming," says the Israeli president.

"I agree it's a difficult burden. But, if you will forgive me, I have two hundred million to govern, while you have only two million."

"Ah," says the Israeli president. "It is true that you are the president of two hundred million, but I am the president of two million presidents!"

I met a Jew who had grown up in a yeshiva and knew large sections of the Talmud by heart.

I met a Jew who was an atheist.

I met a Jew who owned a large clothing store with hundreds of employees, and I met a Jew who was an ardent communist. . . .

It was all the same man.

—ISAAC BASHEVIS SINGER

"Three Jews, Three Opinions"— Even When We're Alone . . .

Marcus, shipwrecked on a deserted island for three years, is finally reached by rescuers.

Proudly, he shows them around the island, pointing out the pastures, the crude irrigation system, the gardens. At the end of the island are two small thatched huts. "And those," he announces, "are the synagogues."

"Two of them?" he is asked. "But you're alone here!"

"Well," he says, "this is the one I pray in— and the other one? I wouldn't go in if you paid me!"

· · · ● · · ·

So Nu, That's It? Never Satisfied

Whether it comes from wandering in the desert, an insatiable thirst for life, or the general conviction that if one is good, two is better (or safer), contentment is typically not part of the Jewish mind-set.

A Jewish mother and her four-year-old were walking along the beach when suddenly a gigantic wave rolled up on the shore, sweeping the little girl out to sea.

"Oh, G-d," lamented the mother, her face toward heaven. "This is my only baby. She is the love, the joy of my life. I have cherished every moment with her. Please, G-d! Bring her back to me and I'll go to synagogue and pray every day!"

Suddenly another gigantic wave rolled up on the beach and deposited the girl back on the sand, safe and sound.

The mother looked up and said, "She had on a hat."

• • ● • •

Fishman got separated from his tour bus in Israel, so he set out to find it.

After shlepping a mile in the boiling heat, he started murmuring, "Water . . . water . . ." The sun baked his skin; the sand caused him to stumble. Just as he was sure he was a goner, a small house appeared on the horizon. Fishman crawled over and scratched at the door. A woman opened it, and Fishman, on his knees, whispered, "water . . . water!"

"Of course!" said the woman, who ran, returning with a glass. "Here!"

Brightening, Fishman stared. "Did you let it run a little?"

Even the righteous need to know when enough is enough.

It's teeming. The rising river threatens the home of Pincus, already standing in water.

A police boat comes by, and the officer shouts, "Pincus, the water's rising. Let us evacuate you!"

Pincus declines. "I trust G-d will deliver me."

After an hour the officer shouts to Pincus, now on the second floor. "There is very little time! Let us evacuate you!"

Pincus declines. "G-d will deliver me."

Finally, an officer in a helicopter shouts at Pincus, on the roof, "Grab the rope, we'll pull you up!"

Pincus again declines, saying, "G-d will deliver me."

Pincus drowns.

In heaven he comes before G-d. "Lord, I've been righteous my whole life, so in my hour of need, where were you?"

G-d sighs. "I sent two boats and a helicopter. That wasn't enough for you?"

Nakhes

Since family, especially children, is the center of Jewish life, should it not follow that all those years of devotion should reap rewards? Right? Of course, right. Pronounced "nockiss" (a little throat clearing on the *ck*) the word means "pleasurable pride." Not just because Junior learned to tie his shoe. Big Pride. Now you can die a happy person. Even better to share your *nakhes* with a friend who hasn't yet heard the news.

Nakhes: *The Daughter*

Mrs. Gold and Mrs. Bloom run into each other in the street after twenty years.

"How's your daughter," inquires Mrs. Gold, "the one who married the surgeon?"

"Divorced," answers Mrs. Bloom.

"Oy."

"Ah, but she married a brilliant attorney."

"Mazel Tov!" (Congratulations).

"They also were divorced. But . . . she's now engaged to a millionaire developer."

Mrs. Gold shakes her head from side to side. "Mmmm mmmm, mmmm. So much *nakhes* from one daughter."

Nakhes: *The Son*

Now it's Mrs. Gold's turn to *shep* (get) a little *nakhes* of her own.

"So tell me, how's your boy Marvin?" asks Mrs. Bloom.

"Only the best doctor in all of North America," says Mrs. Gold. "You must go to him."

"Why? There's nothing wrong with me."

"Listen!" says Mrs. Gold, puffing up with nakhes. "With my son, believe me, you go only once, he'll find something!"

Nakhes: *On Becoming*

It's never too early to prepare.

Mrs. Feinbaum is walking down the street with her two young sons. A passerby asks her how old they are.

"The doctor is three," says Mrs. Feinbaum. "And the lawyer, he's two."

The greatest Jewish tradition is to laugh. The cornerstone of Jewish survival has always been to find humor in life and in ourselves.

—JERRY SEINFELD

Some Comedy Legends: Thanks for the Comfort

THE GREAT DANE

Victor Borge may have been the funniest man ever to walk onto a stage. He was certainly the funniest pianist ever to do so. Through the melding of his comic and musical talents, Borge, a prodigy who debuted with the Danish symphony at age ten, gained a unique place in show business. When the Nazis forced him to flee his homeland, he escaped on the last U.S. passenger ship to leave Scandinavia before the United States entered World War II. In the 1950s his one-man show *Comedy in Music* ran for three years on Broadway. His fans are legion— and surprising. Even Saddam Hussein once requested a video! A recipient of the Medal of Honor, Borge was honored at the Kennedy Center in 1999. He died on December 23, 2000.

He once said, "Laughter is the shortest distance between two people."

• • ● • •

GROUNDBREAKER: MORT SAHL

"Is there any group I haven't offended?" was a common question Mort Sahl would ask audiences. Starting in the fifteis Sahl, who believe it or not once dreamed of going to West Point, broke the mold and led the way for countless comics by losing the formal wear to sweaters and punch lines to monologues of social observations without taboos. The intellectual, whose favorite authors are Twain, Melville, Paine, Shaw, and, yes, Einstein, has a lighter side. He likes to surround himself with electric razors, expensive watches, and sleek sports cars.

> When I was a kid, I wanted to be somebody. And then I found that amusing people is a helluva way to make a living. And now you might say it is the syndrome of the Jews: if you don't laugh you die.
>
> —ALAN KING

• • • ● • •

HAIL TO THEE, MIGHTY CAESAR

Born Isaac Sidney Caesar in 1922 in Yonkers, New York, Sid Caesar will forever be considered an undisputed comic genius for his work in early TV. He accomplished this feat with his extraordinary ear for languages, an unmatched gift for characterization, and a dream team of writers and costars that included Woody Allen, Mel Brooks, Neil Simon, Larry Gelbart, Carl Reiner, Imogene Coca, and Howard Morris. The shy, intellectual Caesar started as a saxophonist but over time made the transition to comedy and hit his stride with the new medium in comedy-variety shows like *Your Show of Shows,* which ran from February 25, 1950, to June 5, 1954. Caesar brought to early television a new kind of comedy: sketch and character humor.

Sid Caesar's Most Beloved Characters and Sketches

"History as She Ain't": Monologues, mime, and satires on TV shows and films, e.g., *From Here to Obscurity*

The Professor: The visiting authority on everything who knew nothing

The Hickenloopers: A husband-and-wife skit with Imogene Coca

The Great Clock of Baverhoff, Bavaria:
Mechanical figures went haywire on the hour

The Italian Opera Star: Gibberish warbling in
Galapacci

Progress Hornsby: Supercool jazz musician

Caesar's verbal acuity was also evident in the
double-talking foreigner and his monologue as a
fly—including sound effects.

THE DOC IS IN

Born on the Fourth of July, Neil Simon, the son of a traveling salesman, holds more records for plays written, hits, and plays adapted to film than any other living playwright. An original screenwriter as well, he holds the Quadruple Crown for awards—in multiples. In addition to a Pulitzer Prize, he has received Tonys, Emmys, and a Screen Writers Guild Award. Since helping to define comedy during the early days of television, this shrewd and hysterical observer of the human condition has written comedic and sensitive masterpieces. A very small sampling includes *Come Blow Your Horn; Barefoot in the Park; The Odd Couple, Sweet Charity; Plaza Suite; The Out-of-Towners; Promises; Promises, Chapter Two; The Sunshine Boys;* and *Lost in Yonkers.* It was during the 1980s that he created his landmark autobiographical trilogy.

On December 10, 1982, at the Ahmanson Theater in Los Angeles, we first met fifteen-year-old Eugene Morris Jerome on an imaginary pitcher's mound by his family's Brooklyn house in *Brighton Beach Memoirs.* The year was 1937. We saw two families struggling to live under the same worn roof during the Depression, with each member trying to "come of age." Eugene's story continues in *Biloxi Blues,* his second coming of age in the army, and once again in *Broadway Bound,* as Eugene comes of (older) age for a third time, launching his writing career and moving beyond the beach. It is within

this extraordinary trilogy of one Jewish family that
we get into the *kishkes* (insides) of us all, in our
hilarity and our humanity.

"YOU MUST BE THAT FUNNY GIRL"
—*Nick Arnstein*

Whether Fanny Brice was mocking "belly dansehs"
or sirens of history with her trademark Yiddish
accent and facial gestures, the first lady of vaudeville
was an original. Not only because she was a
Broadway and radio star (*Baby Snooks*) but also
because Brice, born Fanny Borach in Brooklyn in
1891, was an art expert, costume designer, interior
decorator for stars like Eddie Cantor, Danny Kaye,
and Dinah Shore—and a minor hypnotist. Of her
work, she said: "I never did a Jewish routine that
would offend my race because I depended on my
race for the laughs. In anything Jewish I ever did, I
wasn't standing apart making fun. I was the race,
and what happened to me onstage is what could
happen to my people."

The funny lady, who despite the "Yinglish" shtick
never spoke a word of Yiddish, so fascinated that she
became the subject of two musical Broadway plays
and films, *Funny Girl* and *Funny Lady*, starring the
brilliant Barbra Streisand.

INSPIRATIONS AND ADMIRATIONS

Jewish performers on Jews they have been inspired by or have admired.

Woody Allen: Groucho Marx

Mort Sahl: S. J. Perelman and George S. Kaufman

Roseanne: Lenny Bruce, Jack Benny, Rodney Dangerfield, Totie Fields, Phyllis Diller

Richard Belzer: Lenny Bruce, Jackie Mason

Elayne Boosler: Robert Klein

Red Buttons: Eddie Cantor, W. C. Fields, Fanny Brice

Jerry Seinfeld: Robert Klein

Richard Lewis: Woody Allen, Lenny Bruce

Buddy Hackett: George Burns

David Steinberg: Carly Simon, Bette Midler

The World According to "Him"

> The Talmud is the study of logic. . . . Every time I see a contradiction or hypocrisy in somebody's behavior, I think of the Talmud and build the joke from there.
>
> —Jackie Mason

When Jackie Mason's *The World According to Me!* opened on Broadway in 1986, he became legend. While his "Jews and Gentiles" material evoked some controversy, he told the author, "I see no difference between what I'm doing and anthropological observation. For some Jews it's stereotyping, for anybody else, it's sociology." On one thing we all agree. He's a hit.

> Houses: Go in any gentile home, they hit you with hammers, nails . . . banging. . . . The toilet was once a chair. . . . The second floor was once a chimney. The whole wall was once in Philadelphia. . . . They can put up another house for you in ten seconds. . . . You watch the seven o'clock news, and every single day throughout the Midwest . . . gentile homes are

flying around . . . and the same gentiles are standing there. "What happened to your house?" "It left again."

A Jewish house, if it gets a nick on it . . . two minutes later, there's ninety lawyers and fifty accountants.

• • • ● • • •

Cars: If a gentile car breaks down, in two seconds they're under the car, on top of the car. . . . It becomes an airplane and he flies away. A Jewish car breaks down and you always hear . . . : "It stopped." And the wife always says, "It's your fault." And the husband says, "I know what it is. It's in the hood." She says, "Where's the hood?" He says, "I don't remember."

—JACKIE MASON,
The World According to Me!

• • • ● • • •

"She was the first female stand-up who worked like a man. With chutzpah!"

So said Freddie Roman about Totie Fields, adding, "During one of my Catskill appearances in 1970, Totie was in the audience. After the show, she asked me when I last worked in Las Vegas. 'Never,' I said. 'Yeah? Watch.'

"Totie then called Juliet Prowse's manager, who said, 'I never heard of him.' 'Doesn't matter,' said Totie. 'I hired him for you.'

"When I opened in Las Vegas she brought forty people, including Steve [Lawrence] and Eydie [Gormé], which led to my working with them at Caesar's. This was all due to Totie."

Born in Hartford in 1930, Totie Fields (née Sophie Feldman) got her break in 1962, when she opened for Chubby Checker in Pittsburgh, then hit the big time at the Copacabana in New York, which lead to an appearance on *The Ed Sullivan Show.* Widely regarded as the funniest female in America during the sixties and seventies, after suffering numerous health problems she died on August 2, 1978. Comedy is a rough business. Totie Fields made it a kinder, gentler, and funnier one.

I would escape to New York City; that was the only place on earth where Jews could live, I thought. . . . Where a Jewish comic shrieked properly for a few moments about living in exile in a cruel, cold world, where the only thing that calmed the terror for a while was the joke, the laugh.

—ROSEANNE

MASTERS OF MADCAP

"They were the one act I could never follow," said W. C. Fields. He was referring to the Marx Brothers. And there has been nothing like these zany, comic anarchists before or since. Driven by their mother, Minnie, Chico (Leonard), Harpo (Arthur), Zeppo (Herbert), Gummo (Milton), and of course, Groucho (Julius) made film history.

Can you match the film to the song or antic?

1. *The Cocoanuts* (1925)	A. "Hooray for Captain Spaulding"
2. *Animal Crackers* (1930)	B. "(Whatever It Is) I'm Against It"
3. *Monkey Business* (1931)	C. The boys stow away, crash a party, catch some crooks
4. *Duck Soup* (1933)	D. Chico confuses "viaduct" and "why a duck"
5. *Horse Feathers* (1932)	E. "Lydia, the Tattooed Lady"
6. *At the Circus* (1939)	F. Harpo/Groucho as mirror images

1—D; 2—A; 3—C; 4—F; 5—B; 6—E

And the brothers were as versatile off-screen as on. Groucho corresponded with the literary giants T. S. Eliot, James Thurber, and E. B. White, and was also an expert tennis player. Harpo, who became "mute" when the script for *Home Again* accidentally gave him only a few lines (he pantomimed and it stuck), was a fine watercolor artist. And Chico, in addition to the piano, could play the cornet, violin, and zither.

THE STORYTELLER

Myron Cohen made you feel you were sharing a schnapps with your uncle—while he was feeling fabric in the garment district in New York, which Cohen did. Born in 1902, he quit selling textiles in the forties after realizing his talent for amusing customers could make him a living. Primarily a teller of anecdotes, often in a Yiddish accent (he himself had none), he told stories that were clean, homespun, and fun. Listen . . .

> Two women in the Bronx are hanging clothes to dry.
> One asks, "Have you seen what's going on in Poland?"
> The other replies, "I live in the back—I don't see anything."

CROSS A PESCHKOWSKY WITH A BERLIN

And what you get is one of the most insightful semi-improv teams from 1957 to 1962, otherwise known as Mike Nichols and Elaine May. While both went on to stellar solo career success, when they were a team their humor was character-driven, sometimes with a Jewish "feel." Here's an excerpt from their classic, "Mother & Son" . . .

> Mother (to grown son on phone): I sat by that phone all day Friday, all day Saturday, and all

day Sunday. . . . Your father said to me, "Phyllis, eat something; you'll faint." I said, "No, Harry, no, I don't want my mouth to be full when my son calls me."

By the end of the routine, the son is reduced to baby talk, signing off with "I wuv you, Mommy."

America's Charitable Clown

When, on March 16, 1926, entertainers Rae and Danny Lewis (Levitch) brought a son, Jerry, into the world, chances are someone up there felt it was time to welcome a King of Clowns. And by five, the little heir apparent to Chaplin was out of rehearsal and onstage in the Catskill Mountains.

In 1946, when Jerry suggested that Dean Martin replace another performer during a gig in Atlantic City, show business history was made. Before the team called it quits exactly ten years later, they were the biggest thing since Philco, in clubs, on TV, and in film.

After the split, Jerry Lewis went on to a brilliant and diverse solo career. He is known internationally for his film work on both sides of the camera.

• • • ● • • •

Can you match the Jerry Lewis film with the description?

1. *The Bellboy* (1960)	A. Jekyll/Hyde— with laughter
2. *The Nutty Professor* (1963)	B. Slapstick— spoke only at end
3. *The Family Jewels* (1965)	C. Played it straight as kidnapped talk-show host
4. *The King of Comedy* (1983)	D. Played seven roles, including the inspiredly incompetent Eddie

1—B; 2—A; 3—D; 4—C

The versatile Lewis is as well known for his philanthropy as for his comedy. He has been raising funds for the Muscular Dystrophy Association since 1950, and his Jerry Lewis Labor Day Telethons have been a staple since 1966.

SATIRE IS TRAGEDY PLUS TIME

This was said by the man who didn't live to see his cult status or his style become a model for comics to come. Lenny Bruce, born Leonard Alfred Schneider in 1926, turned comedy into a new venue some called sick. Toward the late fifties Bruce's act moved into controversial areas (e.g., religion and sexuality) that he punctuated with profanity—sometimes switching to Yiddish to confuse police who were observing for "obscenity." After well-publicized arrests, his work suffered, and he died of an overdose in 1966 at age thirty-nine. His legacy was breaking ground for other artists by attacking hypocrisy and censorship. This idiosyncratic comic, who had his hotel rooms painted blue and was obsessed with cleanliness, was immortalized in a Broadway play, *Lenny* (1971), and in a film by the same name in 1974, with the title role played by Dustin Hoffman.

> The only honest art form is laughter, comedy. You can't fake it . . . you can't.
>
> —LENNY BRUCE

A MAN FOR ALL FOLKS

Sam Levinson, the laid-back observer of the American (and Jewish) family scene during the 1950s and '60s, often recounted personal anecdotes. Typical is this piece on the younger generation.

> Momma and Poppa got no joy from us kids. They . . . raised us to the point where we could produce grandchildren. . . .
>
> We were dopes. These are smart. Smart? GENIUSES.
>
> If we went to the park they called us loafers. The baby is . . . dragged because . . . it's good for him. . . .
>
> [He] can't walk yet but there's a bicycle waiting for him.
>
> We missed the best things in life.
>
> We should have been grandchildren.
>
> —SAM LEVINSON,
> *Meet the Folks*

"YOO-HOO, MRS. BLOOM"

This was a signature line of the quintessential Jewish mother, Molly Goldberg, the character written and first broadcast on radio in 1929 by the versatile Gertrude Berg (born Edelstein in 1899). The Goldbergs innovated recurring characters in everyday life. Molly was the problem solver for her husband,

Jake, the children, and Uncle David. And though the Yinglish was fractured—"Vhy don't you buy a bed and slip dere and finished! And dat's bizness? It's slavery—just like in *Oncle Tom's Cabinet!*"—the show presented Jewish life and the problems of urban life in a way that brought pride to its Jewish fans and proved popular for almost twenty years on radio, then on TV from 1949 to 1955.

MR. NICE GUY

"Are you Italian?" he asks an audience member. "You, the one with the flies all around . . . The Jew's laughing, and the black guy just picked his pocket." Not politically correct? True, but then Don Rickles, King of the Put-downs, has been putting 'em down—and away—in clubs and on TV for over fifty years with just this kind of PI ribbing. Although Mr. Warmth, raised in a strictly Orthodox home in New York, probably will never heed his mother's advice to "tell nice stories like Bob Newhart," he has said he is still very pious, very conscious of being Jewish, and considers his humor cathartic, "a satire of attitudes and prejudices."

GILDED GIRL

Gilda Radner was one of *Saturday Night Live*'s 1975 originals, later moving into a film career, often with her husband, Gene Wilder. Despite her short life, her early characters, such as Emily Litella, who gets worked up over Soviet "Jewelry," Lisa Loopner, the teen nerd who sniffles to "The Way We Were," and the newswoman Rosanne Rosanna-Dana, who is fixated on that "stuff" you find in the corner of your eye—live on in reruns and in our hearts.

With Gilda it was "always something,"and her life was made even more meaningful by Gilda's Club, started in 1995, to provide support for cancer patients and their families. Gilda, born in 1946, died of the disease in 1989.

MESHUGGE (CRAZY) BY DESIGN

> For every ten Jews beating their breasts, G-d
> designated one to be crazy and amuse the
> breast-beaters. By the time I was five I knew I
> was that one.
>
> —MEL BROOKS

Brooks, born Melvin Kaminsky in 1926, cut his
comic teeth in the Catskill hotels and as a writer for
Sid Caesar's *Your Show of Shows* in the 1950s. After
he teamed with the brilliant Carl Reiner on the
Two-Thousand-Year-Old Man albums in the sixties,
he made history with films like *The Producers*
(1967), *Blazing Saddles* (1974), *Young Franken-
stein* (1974), and *High Anxiety* (1977). In 2001,
his stage adaptation of *The Producers* garnered more
Tony Awards than any other preceding musical on
Broadway. The versatile Brooks has confessed that
his comic mania comes from anger and fear as a
Jew, as a person, and because of the early loss of his
father. Married for years to Anne Bancroft (born
Italiano), he allowed their son to be baptized, providing he would also be Bar Mitzvahed.

The Universe According to
the Two-Thousand-Year-Old Man:
Reiner and Brooks

Mel Brooks and the legendary Carl Reiner made comic history with their Two-Thousand-Year-Old Man routines, with Brooks as the unimpressed, ancient Jewish man interviewed by Reiner. Listen . . .

Transportation: Fear was the main mode of transportation, you'd see a lion you'd run 200 miles in a minute!

Children: I have over 42,000 . . . and not one comes to visit me.

A Visit from the Folks (peering into his cave): We just want to look at you. . . . No, we can stand. . . . Nah, we ate on the way, on the dinosaur.

Paul Revere: An anti-Semite for yelling, "The Yiddish are coming! The Yiddish are coming!" (though he offered to send Revere's wife an apology when corrected).

• • • ● • •

ANGST TO ART

> "It implies that He doesn't exist, or—if He does—He really can't be trusted. Since coming to this conclusion I have twice been struck by lightning and once forced to engage in conversation with a theatrical agent.
>
> —WOODY ALLEN,
> on whether *Love and Death*
> might be anti-G-d

Born Allen Stewart Konigsberg in 1935, Woody Allen turned angst into an art form, his Jewishness providing some major grist, e.g., his concept of an anti-Semitic talking elevator. In *Annie Hall* (1977), a classic scene shows Alvie Singer (Allen) imagining himself with long coat and earlocks in the eyes of Annie's non-Jewish grandmother followed by a split screen of her "never-get-sick-or-anything" family versus *his* discussing the latest coronary. After writing for others like Sid Caesar and Jack Paar, Allen started stand-up in 1960. His first film, *What's New, Pussycat?* (1965), blended his writing and acting talents. In others, like *Interiors*, *Manhattan*, and *Hannah and Her Sisters*, he developed his unique existential "feel" and love affair with New York, and he has since become one of our most important filmmakers.

Monologue on G-d and Carpeting: My parents
are what you would call Old World. My parents come from Brooklyn, which is the heart
of the Old World. They're very stable,
down-to-earth people who don't approve of
divorce. Their values in life are G-d and carpeting.

I came home on a Sunday, this was a long
time ago. My father's watching *The Ed
Sullivan Show* on television. He's watching the
Indiana Home for the Criminally Insane Glee
Club on *The Ed Sullivan Show.*

My mother's in the corner knitting a
chicken.

And I said I had to get a divorce. My
mother put down her knitting. She got up, and
she went over to the furnace. She opened the
door, and she got in. Took it rather badly I
thought.

—Recorded at Mr. Kelly's in Chicago,
released as "NYU" on *Woody Allen,*
(Colpix, 1964)

• • • ● • • •

"THE COOLEST PERSON ON THE PLANET"

That is how Jack Nicholson described George Burns, who, born Nathan Birnbaum in 1896, began his career at eight with the Pee Wee Quartet at Rozenzweig's Candy Store in New York. He teamed with Gracie Allen in the twenties, and they became one of comedy's most beloved husband-wife acts. In 1950 their radio show moved to TV, airing 229 episodes. After Gracie's death in 1964, Burns continued his trademark act of half-finished songs and jokes, then, at seventy-five, turned movie star, winning an Oscar for *The Sunshine Boys* (1975) and starring in the *Oh God!* films.

A staunch supporter of Jewish causes, Burns was honored at eighty-five, by Ben Gurion University. When he died on March 9, 1996, at one-hundred years, forty-nine days, President Clinton called him "one of the great entertainers of all time."

George is buried next to his beloved Gracie.

The Wit and Wisdom of the Hundred-Year-Old Man: George Burns (1896–1996)

Nice to be here? At my age it's nice to be anywhere.

I get a standing ovation just standing.

I would go out with women my age, but there are no women my age.

On his Oscar: This is all so exciting. I've decided to keep making movies every thirty-six years.

People have asked me what Gracie and I did to make our marriage work. . . . We didn't do anything. . . . The trouble with a lot of people is that they work too hard. . . . They make a business out of it. When you work too hard at a business you get tired; and when you get tired . . . you start fighting; and when you start fighting you're out of business.

Say good night, Gracie.

Without Them,
WOULD THIS WORLD
LAUGH QUITE AS LOUD?

JERRY LEWIS   Jackie Mason

FREDDIE ROMAN   WOODY ALLEN

Marty Allen   Danny Kaye   Carl Reiner

Bernie Allen   Gene Wilder   Fanny Brice

Zero Mostel   Myron Cohen

Totie Fields   Don Rickles

Sid Caesar   Victor Borge   ROSEANNE

Marx Brothers   Robert Klein   Sam Levinson

Lenny Bruce   MORT SAHL   JOE E. LEWIS

Alan King   RED BUTTONS

Buddy Hackett   GEORGE BURNS

Jack Benny   Harvey Korman   Mel Brooks

Jerry Stiller   Rita Rudner   Phil Silvers

Lou Jacoby   GERTRUDE BERG

MOREY AMSTERDAM   Shelley Berman

JERRY SEINFELD   Joey Bishop   Sammy Shore

Jan Murray   Elayne Boosler

Milton Berle   The Stooges   Dick Shawn

Phyllis Diller   Albert Brooks

David Steinberg DAVID BRENNER

Richard Belzer **Jack Carter**

Rodney Dangerfield **Billy Crystal**

MICKEY KATZ Henny Youngman

Andy Kaufman **Shecky Greene**

Mickey Freeman **HOWIE MANDEL**

Jack Gilford Gilda Radner

Ritz Brothers *JOAN RIVERS*

Paul Reiser Ben Blue *Howard Morris*

Richard Lewis Jerry Lester

SOUPY SALES *Allan Sherman* Marcel Marceau

Phil Foster George Jessel

Jon Stewart Madeline Kahn

ELAINE MAY **Benny Rubin**

Al Shean SMITH AND DALE

Weber and Fields **Wayne and Shuster**

Jacob Jacobs LEO FUCHS ADAM SANDLER

Garry Shandling **Selma Diamond**

Bennie Fields *Carol Leifer*

*All have at least one Jewish parent.

47

Entertainment Legends: Who *Nu*?

"I'M DREAMING OF A—" SING, MAMALA!

The two best-selling Christian holiday songs were written by the son of a cantor named Israel Baline, or Irving Berlin, born in 1888 near the Siberian border. An 1893 pogrom brought the family of eight children to New York. The man who, according to Jerome Kern, "has no place in American music. He *is* American music" has written some of our most enduring songs, including the unofficial national anthem "God Bless America." During his 101-year lifetime, he won a plethora of honors for his charitable contributions and his 1,500-plus standards, but perhaps his most enduring legacies are the two most popular Christian holiday songs, "White Christmas" and "Easter Parade." Not bad for a poor Jewish immigrant who never learned to read or write music!

• • • ● • • •

David Brenner once said that he wears the Jewish Star around his neck "in memory of one of the more than one million Jewish children murdered by the Nazis in World War II." When asked if he actually knew any of the youngsters who were killed, his reply was, "I knew every one of them."

TAKE MY WIFE—PLEASE!

This phrase, forever linked to the Undisputed King of the One-Liner, Henny Youngman, came from a real incident that occurred when his wife walked in at the last minute requesting tickets for *The Kate Smith Show,* on which he was appearing. He said, "Take my wife—please! Get rid of her!" and it became the only joke he actually claimed he created. Youngman also launched Abbott and Costello to stardom when he suggested they replace him on the show in 1938. With the one-liner as his stock-in-trade, Youngman, nearing seventy, became the first comic enlisted for *Dial-A-Joke* by the New York Telephone Company in 1974. *Who nu?*

• • • ● • • •

SWING KING BREAKS COLOR BARRIER

Benny Goodman, who received music lessons at a local Chicago synagogue, made history at the Palomar Ballroom in L.A. on August 21, 1935, when cheering youngsters surrounded the bandstand during a swinging arrangement of "Sugar Foot Stomp"—and the Swing Era was born! Most people know that the Swing King was equally at home playing Mozart. Less known is that the Benny Goodman Quartet, with Gene Krupa on drums, Teddy Wilson on piano, and the vibraphonist Lionel Hampton, made a first dent in the color barrier. Hampton has said, "The Quartet was the forerunner of getting Jackie Robinson into baseball." Goodman was considered America's number one musician by the musicologist Hal Davis. When the King of Swing toured the USSR in 1962, one reporter quipped, "Khrushchev would trade three Sputniks for a Russian Benny Goodman!"

THE YIDDISH HELEN HAYES

Molly Picon, the legendary Yiddish theater star who crossed over in English vehicles such as *Milk and Honey* (1961), had the only Yiddish swimming pool in the world: "At three feet the pool side sign said, 'A *mecha'yeh* [a pleasure]', at five, '*Oy vay*, [it's getting a little deep in here],' and at ten feet, '*Gevalt*'[HEELLPP!]"

An ardent Jewish philanthropist, Picon once said about entertaining at displaced persons' camps after World War II: "We met people who hadn't laughed in seven years and who laughed for the first time. It gave them a sense of normalcy again, to come together and see who was alive."

In 1985 Molly Picon, approaching ninety, received one of the first Goldie Awards from the Congress for Jewish Culture for her contributions to the Jewish performing arts.

Betty Joan Perske, better known as acting legend Lauren Bacall, not only married Hollywood royalty—Bogie and Jason Robards—but comes from Yiddish *Yichus* (a good background). Her first cousin is former Israeli Prime Minister Shimon Peres.

DID YOU KNOW THAT . . . ?

Danny Kaye (born David Kaminsky on January 18, 1913, in Brooklyn) was famous as much for his work with UNICEF as for his films like *The Secret Life of Walter Mitty* (1947). He was also:

1. the ping-pong champ of Beverly Hills in the sixties

2. a founder and part owner of the Seattle Mariners

3. a superb Chinese cook who would sometimes replace the chef at a San Francisco eatery

4. a licensed jet pilot

5. a (hilarious) conductor appearing with orchestras such as the Israeli Philharmonic— yet could not read music.

• • • ● • • •

Judy Holliday was a *tuvim* gift. In fact, the Jewish actress took her last name from her real one, Tuvim, which is the Hebrew word for "holiday." The brilliant comedienne who made us laugh and broke our hearts with her "dumb blonde" performances in vehicles like *Born Yesterday*

(1950) and *Bells Are Ringing* (1960) was actually
a genius, with an IQ of 172! Her gilded career was
cut short when she died in 1965 in her early forties of breast cancer.

• • • ● • • •

"When I'm in trouble, under pressure, I fall
back on being old and Jewish. I rattle phlegm. . . .
I feel good." This was said by the TV, stage, and
film star Billy Crystal. The comic, actor, and
impressionist who helped rejuvenate *Saturday
Night Live* with his amazing mimicry (including
the classic "Fernando" and the word "Mahvelous")
came by his bittersweet "ear" early. "We had
swinging seders," he once said, referring to the
involvement in jazz of his uncle Milt Gabler and
his father. His uncle founded Commodore
Records, and his dad managed Gabler's shop in
Manhattan, so guests included W. C. Handy and
Billie Holiday. Crystal also created the first openly
gay character on TV in the spoof *Soap* from 1977
to 1981.

• • • ● • • •

"Come to Papa, *Bubbeleh*" was a line from one of Mickey Katz's English-Yiddish parodies. Born in 1909, the musician-comedian who "Yinglishized" works like *The Barber of Shlemiel* and *Little Red Rosenberg* was not only a brilliant talent in his own right but papa to Joel Grey and grandpapa to Jennifer! Once, after his opening number, an audience member stood and said, "Hey, Katz, I saw your boy Joel last night in *Cabaret*. He's better than you."

"How can you say that? You haven't seen me do anything yet," Katz replied.

"I've seen enough already," said the woman.

Katz was sincerely proud of his spawn.

THE SUNSHINE BOYS

The Neil Simon hit about reuniting two aging ornery vaudevillians, Lewis and Clark, harked back to the actual comedy team of Smith and Dale. The team brought down houses using Jewish dialect from the early 1900s through the '60s TV era with old-time routines like "Dr. Kronkheit" (sickness). Listen . . .

Smith: Are you a doctor?

Dale: I'm a doctor.

Smith: I'm dubious.

Dale: I'm glad to know you, Mr. Dubious.

Smith: . . . I saw another doctor. He said I had snoo in my blood.

Dale: Snoo? What's snoo?

Smith: Nothing. What's snoo with you?

The two also argued endlessly onstage. When Smith saw Neil Simon's *The Sunshine Boys*, he recognized their gestures (chest poking, spitting in the face) and referred to himself and Dale as being "Simonized."

ONE PUNNY GUY

> I am indeed the worst singer in the world . . .
> and that's why it's so important that the
> musical background and the chorus behind
> me should sound beautiful. . . . So the effect
> is something like this: You're looking into
> Tiffany's most elegant show window, and in
> the window is a black velvet pillow, and right
> in the middle of the pillow is an onion.
> That's me.
>
> —ALLAN SHERMAN

Here are a few of his song-parody gems . . .

"Sarah Jackman" ("Frère Jacques")

"My Zelda" ("Matilda")

"Gimme Jack Cohen and I Don't Care"
("Jimmy Crack Corn")

"Won't you Come Home, Disraeli?" ("Bill
Bailey")

"Glory, Glory, Harry Lewis" ("Battle Hymn
of the Republic")

And of course, "Hello, Muddah; Hello,
Fadduh," to "Dance of the Hours"

In August 1962 his album *My Son the Folk Singer* was released and became one of the biggest hits of all time. Camelot President John F. Kennedy was once overheard singing "Sarah Jackman, how's by you" in the lobby of the Carlisle Hotel in New York.

• • • ● • • •

And while we're on the subject . . . Allan Sherman's first important booking was in January 1963 at the Pasadena Civic Auditorium. It was also Harpo Marx's last, much to the shock of the audience when it was announced after Harpo did his act of silent sight gags and harp playing. While Sherman was still choking with emotion, Harpo—entirely unexpectedly—walked back onstage to a tremendous ovation, went to the mike, and broke his professional silence, expressing his gratitude, moving on to reminiscences, and then rambling on—and on—and on—which brought down the house. *Who nu?*

• • • ● • • •

Did You Know That . . . ?

One of our most gifted and sensitive clowns, Zero Mostel, (Samuel Joel/Simcha Yoel Mostel), born February 28, 1915, made roles like Tevye (*Fiddler on the Roof*), Pseudolus (*A Funny Thing Happened on the Way to the Forum*), and Max Bialystock (*The Producers*) legendary. What you may not know is this:

1. He took the name Zero in 1942 to signify, "Here's a man who's made something of nothing."

2. His zaniness off-screen was legendary. He once shaved the actor Sam Jaffe in a restaurant using the cream off some shortcake.

3. He was a talented artist who felt painting was more creative than acting, because you start with an empty canvas. He also collected Coptic art and Peruvian textiles.

4. He was a leading intellectual and expert on theater, lecturing at Harvard in 1962.

HERE ARE FIVE THINGS YOU PROBABLY NEVER KNEW ABOUT THE DIVINE MISS M— BETTE MIDLER

1. The Honolulu-born funny lady got her big break in 1970 at the Continental Baths—a gay Turkish bath—in New York City.

2. She was named after Bette Davis, her mother thinking the actress pronounced it "Bet" instead of "Betty."

3. Offstage, she's really a square. She lives unpretentiously in a calm atmosphere with her husband and daughter.

4. She's a hausfrau who is obsessive about cleaning—a chore she often does herself.

5. Her wacky portrayals onstage have included: a giant hot dog and a female King Kong.

• • • ● • • •

MASTER MAGICIAN!

Eerie that the greatest magician and escape artist of all time, the Hungarian-born Harry Houdini (Ehrich Weisz, changed to Weiss by immigration officials), the third child of a Rabbi, was to die from peritonitis at age fifty-two on Halloween Day. Eerier yet, for ten years after his death, his wife, Bess, attempted to contact him through the code phrase "Believe, Rosabelle, believe!" but never heard from him. According to the science fiction writer Isaac Asimov, when the pallbearers lifted Houdini's coffin onto their shoulders, one of them stage-whispered to another, "What if he managed to get out?" To this day people keep trying to find out. The good news: Also on Halloween, but in 1975, Houdini's pioneering accomplishments in film earned him a star on Hollywood Boulevard. In 1918 he became a movie star in *The Master Mystery*. Soon after, he set up his own Picture Corporation, for which he wrote and starred in *The Man from Beyond* and *Haldane of the Secret Service*. The magician had a few other talents as well. Four years after the Wright Brothers' historic flight, Houdini made his first. And on March 16, 1910, he became the first person to fly successfully in Australia.

Very little could throw the master except . . .

About seventy years ago at a charity event, Houdini announced a new trick. "I shall place in my mouth a dozen needles and a loose piece of thread. Without using my hands, and in less than one second, I will thread all the needles." Looking over the audience for a volunteer to testify that nothing was hidden, he rejected the celebs, choosing a small man in an aisle seat. "Do you see any needles or thread hidden under my tongue?" Houdini asked the man. The man looked into Houdini's mouth but said not a word. "Speak right up. Tell the audience what you see."

"Pyorrhea!" quipped the little man.

In a crowd of sixteen hundred, Houdini had the misfortune of choosing Groucho Marx, whom he didn't recognize without the grease-paint mustache! The audience laughed for two whole minutes.

• • • ● • • •

Jack Benny was a wanderer. The funny man who was such a master of timing he could get a laugh by merely staring at an audience and folding his arms was, off-screen, a little—helpless. Everyone fretted over him, even total strangers. For example, he had a habit of wandering off in airports to buy a paper or magazine, then losing his gate. Fortunately, someone—usually a guard or a pretty girl—would invariably befriend the hapless comedian and "return" him on time.

MR. TELEVISION

Milton Berle, born Milton Berlinger on July 12, 1908, was deservedly dubbed Mr. Television because his shtick on *Texaco Star Theater* from 1948 to 1953 "sold more television sets than Montgomery Ward," according to the *People* magazine TV reviewer David Hiltbrand. Known for his wisecracks, the comic also became famous for his bits in drag. What you may *not* know is this was sparked by a real incident. It seems he adopted the gear to sneak into the Barbizon, a women's residence in New York. Adorned as an "attractive" roomer, he managed to get to his lady's room. Never a shirker, while a student and vaudeville performer, the fifteen-year-old Berle earned extra bucks sitting for the son of his fellow vaudevillian Belle Montrose, who had a babe in need of care backstage—the two-year-old Steve Allen! *Who nu?*

• • • ◗ • • •

Eddie Cantor, born Isidore Itzkowitz, in New York on January 31, 1892, who reached the peak of his popularity through radio in the 1930s and '40s, adopted the song, "Ida, Sweet as Apple Cider" as his theme song in honor of his wife, Ida Tobias. An inveterate fund-raiser, he was affectionately called the *shnorrer* (beggar) in Israel for his tireless efforts on that country's behalf. When President Franklin D. Roosevelt asked Cantor to organize a drive to raise funds to fight polio, the comic-singer suggested asking each donor for only ten cents and coined the term the March of Dimes, which became the program's slogan.

FUNNY, THEY DON'T "LOOK" JEWISH

You may be surprised to know that a large number of celebrities, particularly from yesteryear, were/are Jewish or had one Jewish parent. *Who nu*?

Lauren Bacall
   [Betty Joan Perske]

Bert Lahr
   [Irving Lahrheim]

Mama "Cass" Elliot
   [Ellen Cohen]

Paulette Goddard
   [Pauline Marion
   Levy]

Edward G. Robinson
   [Emmanuel
   Goldenberg]

Theda Bara
   [Theodosia
   Goodman]

Jeff Chandler
   [Ira Grossel]

Winona Ryder
   [Winona Horowitz]

Melvyn Douglas
   [Melvyn
   Hesselberg]

Simone Signoret
   [Simone Kaminker]

Artie Shaw
   [Arthur Jacob
   Arshawsky]

John Garfield
   [Julius Garfinkle]

Lee J. Cobb
   [Leo Jacob]

Gene Barry
   [Eugene Klass]

David Copperfield
   [David Katkin]

Peter Lorre
   [Laszlo Löwenstein]

Dyan Cannon
   [Samille Diane
   Friesen]

Tony Martin
   [Alvin Morris]

Jill St. John
   [Jill Oppenheim]

André Previn
   [André Prewin]

Soupy Sales
   [Milton Supman]

Arthur Murray
   [Arthur Teichman]

Gene Simmons
   [Chaim Witz]

Ed Wynn
   [Isaiah Edwin
   Leopold]

Who Nu? Did You Nu? A Few Quizzes (And, Yes, Now You May Smack Me)
Out of the Closet: Jewish Television Characters

Though *The Goldbergs* was popular in the early fifties, TV wasn't showcasing Jewish characters. In fact, a test audience found *The Mary Tyler Moore Show*, "too Jewish" but the show became a legend and spun off another successful series with a Jewish title character (played by the non-Jew Valerie Harper). Since then, we've seen Seinfeld and Paul Buchman (Paul Reiser) take center stage.

Match the character to the show.

Character	Show
1. Lilith Sternin	A. *The Wonder Years*
2. Sylvia Fine	B. *Taxi*
3. Alex Rieger	C. *Murphy Brown*
4. Miles Silverberg	D. *Brooklyn Bridge*
5. Brenda Morgenstern	E. *The Nanny*
6. Paul Pfeiffer	F. *The Dick Van Dyke Show*
7. Sophie Berger	G. *Rhoda*
8. Buddy Sorrell	H. *Cheers*

1—H (Bebe Neuwirth); 2—E (Renee Taylor);
3—B (Judd Hirsch); 4—C (Grant Shaud);
5—G (Julie Kavner); 6—A (Josh Saviano);
7—D (Marion Ross); 8—F (Morey Amsterdam)

What Was It Before? . . .

"Mr. Poisson," says the secretary, "your mother, Mrs. Fish, is calling."

"Mama, are you okay? Sofia and I were worried when you didn't show up at our condo-warming party last night."

"The lobby's gorgeous," says Mrs. Fish.

"But, Mama, if you were there, why didn't you come up?" asks Poisson, puzzled.

"I forgot your name."

Not long ago anybody who wanted to be "somebody" changed his or her ethnic name. Today more are keeping them, but the late, great Walter Matthau may still have lopped a little from Matuschanskavasky!

Match the stage with the real name.

Stage Name	Real Name
1. Tony Curtis	A. Leonard Hacker
2. Jackie Mason	B. Bernard Schwartz
3. Sophie Tucker	C. Sonia Kalish
4. Buddy Hackett	D. Irwin Kniberg
5. Jerry Lewis	E. Joseph Levitch
6. Beatrice Arthur	F. Yacov Maza
7. Alan King	G. Bernice Frankel

1—B; 2—F; 3—C; 4—A; 5—E; 6—G; 7—D

Nyuk-nyuk!

This exclamation—along with slaps and pokes—was a trademark of those Kings of Low Comedy, the Three Stooges. Moe Howard and Larry Fine (Louis Fineberg) were the team's anchors, while the third spot was most often played by Moe's real-life brothers, Shemp and Curly (Samuel and Jerome). How much do you know these Jewish *nudniks* personally? Take this true-false quiz.

1. Moe's bowl-shaped mane was a wig.   T F

2. Moe's yanking cost Larry most of his hair.   T F

3. Curly was naturally bald.   T F

4. Moe was always late, while Larry was usually early.   T F

5. Curly was a superb ballroom dancer.   T F

5—T

4—F: The reverse. Larry's chronic lateness drove Moe crazy.

3—F: He had plush wavy brown hair that he clipped weekly.

2—T

1—F: It was his own, he normally wore it back, shook it down for films.

"Sometimes, when you look Andy in the eyes, you get a feeling somebody else is driving."—David Letterman

Few comics have aroused as much speculation as Andy Kaufman. Acts or oddities, how much do you know about him?

1. Which classic book did he once read to an audience?

2. Name the cartoon character he lip-synched to.

3. In 1979 he invited a Carnegie Hall audience to do what?

4. He challenged women in what sport?

5. His lounge lizard alter ego was who?

1—*The Great Gatsby*
2—Mighty Mouse
3—Eat milk and cookies at the New York School of Printing
4—Wrestling
5—Tony Clifton

They Said (or Did) It—You Laughed

Match the line or shtick with the performer.

Line or Shtick	Performer/Character
1. "Now cut that out!"	A. Jerry Seinfeld
2. "Enter, whoever!"	B. Milton Berle
3. "Good evening, ladies and germs."	C. Emily Litella
4. "What's the story there?"	D. Jack Benny
5. "You look mahvelous."	E. Billy Crystal
6. "Everybody gotta be someplace."	F. Joe E. Lewis
7. "Never mind!"	G. Marty Allen
8. "Hello, Dere!	H. Molly Goldberg
9. Pea soup coming to a boil	I. Don Rickles
10. "Post time"	J. Myron Cohen
11. "You hockey puck!"	K. Jack Gilford

1—D; 2—H; 3—B; 4—A; 5—E; 6—J;
7—C; 8—G; 9—K; 10—F; 11—I

Play It Again, Mamala

Match these music legends with something or someone they sang or composed about, played or worked with, or was known as:

1. Mel Torme	A. He had "High Hopes"
2. Burt Bacharach	B. Wasn't crazy about "Short People"
3. Carole King	C. "The Velvet Fog"
4. Sammy Kahn	D. Scored "The Sting"
5. Dinah Shore	E. It's [Never] Too Late" for *Tapestry* Legend
6. Marvin Hamlisch	F. Hit it with the Tijuana Brass
7. Randy Newman	G. "See the U.S.A. in your Chevrolet"
8. Herb Alpert	H. Dionne Warwick

1–C; 2–H; 3–E; 4–A; 5–G; 6–D; 7–B; 8–F

More What Was It Before?

Match the stage name with the real name.

Stage Name	Real Name
1. Beverly Sills	A. Jacob Cohen
2. Eddie Cantor	B. Isidore Itzkowitz
3. Red Buttons	C. Leonard Rosenthal
4. Rodney Dangerfield	D. Jerome Silverman
5. Tony Randall	E. Lyova Haskell Rosenthal
6. Gene Wilder	F. Belle Silverman
7. Jack Benny	G. Shirley Schrift
8. Danny Kaye	H. Aaron Chwatt
9. Hal Linden	I. Harold Lipshitz
10. Robert Merrill	J. Fivel Feldman
11. Lee Grant	K. Sidney Liebowitz
12. Steve Lawrence	L. Benjamin Kubelsky
13. Mike Todd	M. Albert Einstein
14. Phil Foster	N. Moishe Miller
15. Albert Brooks	O. Avron Goldbogen
16. Jason Alexander	P. Jay Scott Greenspan
17. Shelley Winters	Q. David Kaminsky

1—F; 2—B; 3—H; 4—A; 5—C; 6—D;
7—L; 8—Q; 9—I; 10—N; 11—E; 12—K;
13—O; 14—J; 15—M; 16—P; 17—G

The Jewish Panther

The comic Peter Sellers, born to a Jewish mother in Southsea, England, was best known for his bumbling Inspector Clouseau in the Pink Panther series. Clouseau was based on Captain Webb, the first to swim the English Channel to France. Sellers also created many unforgettable characters in his films.

Match these.

Films	Characters
1. *The Naked Truth* (1958)	A. Quizmaster, sportsman, policeman, bureaucrat
2. *The Mouse That Roared* (1959)	B. crazy shrink
3. *Dr. Strangelove,* etc. (1964)	C. Jewish lawyer-hippie
4. *What's New Pussycat* (1965)	D. Grand duchess, army commander, PM
5. *I Love You Alice B. Toklas* (1968)	E. English officer, German scientist, U.S. president
6. *Murder by Death* (1976)	F. Dim-witted gardener
7. *Being There* (1979)	G. Chinese detective

1–A; 2–D; 3–E; 4–B; 5–C; 6–G; 7–F

Laughs Across the Ponds: A Sampling

As Jews have wandered, so has their humor spread from country to country.

Can you match the stars with the country that made them famous?

Performer	Country
1. Bud Flanagan	A. Soviet Union or Russia
2. George Voskovec	B. England
3. Max Pallenberg	C. Czechoslovakia
4. Arkady Raikin	D. India
5. Ron Moody	E. Germany
6. Misha Belenky	F. Israel
7. David Abraham	
8. Ezra	
9. Marty Feldman	

1—B; 2—C; 3—E; 4—A; 5—B; 6—A; 7—D; 8—F; 9—B

So . . . did you *nu*?

Without Them,
WOULD THIS WORLD IGNITE
QUITE SO MUCH PASSION?

EDWARD G. ROBINSON   Paul Muni

TONY CURTIS   LUISE RAINER

Dustin Hoffman   Goldie Hawn

Walter Matthau   **Henry Winkler**

Lauren Bacall   Eli Wallach   *Edward Asner*

Judd Hirsch   **Mandy Patinkin**

James Caan   Tony Randall

Rhea Perlman   JACK ALBERTSON   Topol

Leonard Nimoy   Peter Sellers   *Beatrice Arthur*

MARTIN BALSAM   BERT LAHR   Jeff Goldblum

MARTIN LANDAU   Jack Klugman

HARVEY FIERSTEIN   Linda Lavin   **Sam Jaffe**

Judy Holliday   Ed Wynn   Lee Grant

Richard Dreyfuss   *Mel Blanc*

HERB EDELMAN   JEAN CARROLL   **Molly Picon**

SIMONE SIGNORET   Robert Clary

Laurence Harvey   *John Garfield*

Jill St. John   Lee J. Cobb

Gene Barry   *Peter Lorre*

Paulette Goddard   Lainie Kazan

Theda Bara   JEFF CHANDLER

Luther Adler   Winona Ryder
Melvyn Douglas   Kirk Douglas
DYAN CANNON   Michael Douglas
Elliott Gould   Shelley Winters
Paul Newman   David Opatoshu
SARAH BERNHARDT
Alan Arkin   Adam Arkin   Estelle Getty
NANCY WALKER   Efrem Zimbalist, Jr.
Michael Landon   Menashe Skulnik
Herschel Bernardi   Stella Adler
HARRY GOZ   Carol Kane   Lorne Greene
George Segal   Lee Strasberg
Susan Strasberg   Joel Grey
JENNIFER GREY   Gwyneth Paltrow
Alicia Silverstone   RON SILVER
David Duchovny   Howard Da Silva
Yasmine Bleeth   NOAH WYLE   HARVEY KEITEL
Debra Winger   Julianna Margulies
Fyvush Finkel   Jason Alexander
Ron Moody   Hank Azaria   RICHARD BENJAMIN
Michele Lee   Sam Levene   Philip Loeb

*All have at least one Jewish parent.

So, How Are You? Don't Ask!

Greeting: How are you?
Answer (non-Jewish): Fine.
Answer (Jewish): How should I be?

For many Jews, including the author, it is quite normal to assume that a splinter in the toe could be an early warning sign. Whether this is because "Guess who died last night" often follows "Hello" or because we have a morbid fear of the evil eye smiting us, I have rarely met a Jew who feels good—or will admit to it.

The Italian says, "I'm tired and thirsty. I must have wine."
The Scotsman says, "I'm tired and thirsty. I must have Scotch."
The Russian says, "I'm tired and thirsty. I must have vodka."
The Jew says, "I'm tired and thirsty. I must have diabetes."

And the Poster Comic Is Richard Lewis . . .

This self-proclaimed hypochondriac blames heredity, claiming his grandparents were "depressed-again"

Jews with a bumper sticker that read, "I'd rather be weeping." According to Lewis, "I've always been a hypochondriac. When I was a little boy, I used to eat M&M's one by one with a glass of water."

• • • ● • •

Glick: So, Fish, how are you today?

Fish: Oy, I've got so many aches that if a new one came it's a two-week wait before I can make an appointment to worry about it.

• • • ● • •

Max and Shloime were having a glass of tea.

"Did you hear about Mendel Tishman?" asks Shloime.

"You mean Mendel with the goiter?"

"That's the one."

"And the liver condition with the tic?"

"That's him," says Shloime.

"And the yellow skin with the head always bobbing? So, what's to hear?"

"He died."

"Oy!" says Max. "Such a healthy man!"

• • • ● • •

Rifkin: Doctor, please tell me I'm not a well man.

Doctor: Come, Morris. What kind of attitude is that?

Rifkin: Listen, I'd hate to feel like this if I'm well.

I never worry about things I could actually *get*, like from smoking, but I'll be watching TV and they'll be talking about a disease that only seventy-five-year-old Turkish men get, and I'll have every symptom.

—FRAN LEBOWITZ,
in response to a question about her
hypochondria asked by Jon Winokur
in his *Portable Curmudgeon*

An old Jewish woman calls Mount Sinai and gets the receptionist. "I vant who gives the information about the patients, because I need the whole story, soup to nuts."

"Well, madam, that's a very unusual request, but I'll see what I can do."

After a few minutes an authoritative voice comes on. "Are you the woman who is calling about a patient?"

"Yes, darling! I'd like to know all the information about Dora Fleigel. Everything. A to Z. She's in Room 408."

"Hmmm. Fein, Fingle, Fleigel . . . Fleigel—oh yes, Mrs. Fleigel, here it is. Well, she's doing very well. Today her tests are normal, her scans are clear, her blood pressure is down, and she's scheduled to be discharged Tuesday."

"Tuesday! Oy! Denks G-d! Such vonderful vonderful news!"

"From your enthusiasm, I take it you're close to the patient," asked the man.

"Close! Vat close? I *am* the patient! My doctor don't tell me nothing!"

• • • • ● • • •

A Classic

An elderly man goes to the doctor complaining of aches and pains. After a thorough examination, the doctor gives him a clean bill of health. "Hymie, you're in fine shape for an eighty-year-old. After all, I'm not a magician. I can't make you any younger."

"Listen, Doctor, who asked you to make me younger? What I want is to grow older!"

Shnorrers and *Alrightniks*

*C*hutzpah gilt!* (Nerve succeeds!) says a Yiddish
proverb. And both these "types," who are at
opposite ends of the *shekel* (coin), share plenty of
chutzpah! Listen . . .

THE SHNORRER

"So, if you had a bad week, why should I suffer?"
says the *shnorrer* (beggar) in *Fiddler on the Roof*.
How was the *shnorrer* different from other beggars?
To the *shnorrer*, mooching, panhandling, and chis-
eling were an art, a craft, a profession with a noble
role in the community. Without the *shnorrer* to give
charity to, how could a Jew rack up good deeds?

A *shnorrer* came to the Bloom's back door on
his weekly rounds.
"I haven't even a *shekel* in the house," apolo-
gized Mrs. Bloom. "Come back tomorrow."
"Tomorrow?" The *shnorrer* frowned. "Okay,
this once only. But don't let it happen again.
I've lost a fortune extending credit."

• • • ● • •

Every Saturday morning for years the *shnorrer*
appeared at the rich man's house for sumptuous

blintzes (crepes) and cherry sauce. On this particular Saturday, he brought with him a young stranger.

The host, put out, asked, "Who is this?"

"Meet Mendel, my new son-in-law," replied the *shnorrer*. "I promised to give him board the first year."

• • • ● • •

Every Wednesday Yankel the *shnorrer* collects from Epstein—except today.

"I've had terrible troubles," says Epstein. "I invested in the egg market. Not one hen laid. I lost a fortune. My wife got so upset, I sent her to a specialist, who suggested a rest cure at a fancy resort. As it's cold there, I had to buy her an expensive down blanket—"

Yankel gasps. "Wait. This you did with my money!"

THE ALRIGHTNIK

They're in every culture. The French call them *nouveau riche*. And among Jews, too, some have been known to "put on airs" after making a few dollars. But, in typical fashion, Jews deal with *alrightniks* best—with humor. Even if it pokes fun at the pious.

A Classic

Morty made a killing in the stock market, so he thought it befitting to buy a yacht and a fancy captain's uniform with white jacket, hat, and epaulets. One Sunday he invited Mama and Papa from the Bronx for a trip.

"Some yacht, huh? So, what do you think of your son now?"

"Very nice," murmured Mama.

"Yeah," said Papa."Nice. . . ."

"See?" Morty said, pointing to his uniform. "I'm a regular captain now!"

Mama and Papa exchanged glances.

"Well," said Morty, "You don't seem very impressed."

"Morty, darling," said Mama. "By Papa you're a captain, by me you're a captain—but believe me, sonny, by a captain, you're no captain!"

• • • ● ● •

No expense was spared at the Buchman Bar Mitzvah, from the ice statues to the life-size sculpture of the Bar Mitzvah boy in chopped liver next to the mammoth buffet table. The proud mama turns to her unimpressed cousin. "So, what do you think of the gorgeous statue of my Brucie?"

"I've never seen anything like it," he says, unable to resist. "Who did it? Lipschitz or Rothenstyne?"

"Rothenstyne, of course." She sniffed. "Lipschitz only works in whitefish."

• • • ● • •

During one service in a wealthy synagogue, the Rabbi got carried away. Falling on hands and knees, forehead to floor, he said, "Oh G-d, before Thee I am nothing."

The cantor, not to be outdone, also got down, forehead to wood, and said, "Oh G-d, before Thee I am nothing."

Seeing this, Levy, a tailor in the fourth row, left his seat, walked up the aisle, fell to his knees, forehead to floor, and he, too, said, "Oh G-d, before Thee I am nothing."

With this, the cantor elbows the Rabbi and sniffs. "Look who thinks he's nothing!"

A *Shtikl Mishegoss* (A Little Bit o' Nonsense)

In this era of political correctness, the following are based upon trite stereotypes that may no longer exist or never did. And even if they did, we must still ask whether we should use them for the trivial purpose of evoking a smile, a guffaw. So, for those who are offended, I stand pelted with matzah balls. For the rest—enjoy!

JEWISH COUNTRY-WESTERN SONGS

1. "I Was One of the Chosen People (Till She Chose Somebody Else)"

2. "Stand by Your *Mensch*"

3. "I Balanced Your Books but You're Breaking My Heart"

4. "When She Said 'Shalom' I Knew She Meant 'Goodbye'"

5. "Mamas, Don't Let Your Ungrateful Sons Grow Up to Be Cowboys (When They Could Take Over the Hardware Store That Your *Zayde* (Grandpa) Broke His Back to Start, Which They're Turning Their Backs on Now)"

WHO WANTS TO BE A JEWISH MILLIONAIRE? . . . WE'RE TALKING "REAL" MONEY

$125,000

Jews spend vacations

A. Visiting Cathedrals
B. Camping
C. Mountaineering
D. Discussing their last vacation and where they'll spend the next

$250,000

No Jew has ever

A. Become a madam
B. Submitted to unnecessary surgery
C. Gone bathing without a cap
D. Removed the back of a TV

$500,000

There are no Jews living in

A. El Paso
B. Lacosta
C. Sin
D. Trailer parks

$1,000,000

A good child's pet must be

A. Gentle
B. Housebroken
C. Protective
D. Stuffed

FINAL ANSWERS? If you answered D, have I got a tax shelter for you!

IF THEY HAD JEWISH MOTHERS

Paul Revere's: "British, Yiddish! No son of mine rides horses to G-d knows where at midnight."

Mona Lisa's: "All that money on braces and that's the smile we get?"

Michelangelo's: "Do you have any idea how hard it is to get that *shmutz* (dirt) off the ceiling?"

Thomas Edison's: "Of course I'm proud you invented the lightbulb! Now turn it off and go to bed. I'll just sit here in the dark."

FAMOUS JEWISH MOVIES

1. *Gonif* with the Wind*—Ashley Wilkes tries to take over Tara through a forged deed. (*Thief)

2. *Shnorrer* Rae*—Sally Field claims union benefits after she runs back to New York with the organizer to dedicate her life to making gefilte fish. (*Beggar, chiseler)

3. *Bridge over the River Kvetch**—Extras complain that whistling that theme song dries out their mouths and cracks their lips. (*Whine)

4. *The Matzah Candidate*—Frank Sinatra is brainwashed into thinking it's always Passover.

HOW TO TELL IF YOU'RE A JEWISH REDNECK

1. Your belt buckle is bigger than your yarmulke.

2. You think "KKK" is the symbol for really really Kosher.

3. You light Sabbath candles with a cigarette.

4. You think a Hora is a high-priced call girl.

5. You don't ride on the holidays because your car is up on blocks.

6. When someone shouts *L'Chaim!* you shout "L'Howdy!"

"Wisdom" from Chelm

M ention Chelm ("ch" pronounced "k"—with a fur ball in your throat) to a Jew and you'll hear titters. Although there were real Chelms in Poland, in tales, Chelm is a legendary town filled with endearing simpletons suffering from logic that is so literal it's dim-witted. Other cultures have their Chelms: Gotham, in England, Abdera in Greece, and there's TV's Golden Girl Rose Nylund's St. Olaf!

Two wise men of Chelm were out for a walk when suddenly it began to rain.

"Quick," said one man. "Open your umbrella."

"It won't help," said his friend." My umbrella is full of holes."

"Then why bring it in the first place?"

"I didn't think it would rain!"

• • • ● • •

The Rabbi of Chelm and his student stayed at an inn. The student asked the servant to wake him for an early train. Not wishing to disturb the Rabbi, the student, in his haste, put on the rabbinical gabardine. On the train, he was shocked when he looked at himself in the compartment mirror.

"Oy, what a *shlemiel* (idiot) that servant is!" he shrieked. "I asked him to wake me, instead he woke the Rabbi!"

• • • ● • •

Hershel, the milkman of Chelm, was making his rounds one dawn when a stranger rides up, jumps off his wagon and *klops* (slaps) his face.

"So there, Yossel!" he says, satisfied.

After the pain subsided, Hershel gets hysterical with laughter.

"And what's so funny?" asks the stranger, getting ready to *klop* again.

"The joke's on you," says the milkman. "I'm not Yossel!"

A farmer in his wagon picked up a peddler from Chelm who was carrying a heavy bundle on his shoulder. The peddler sat down beside the farmer but kept his bundle on his shoulders.

"Why don't you put your bundle down?" asked the farmer.

"It's nice enough your horse is shlepping me," said the peddler. "Does he have to shlep my bundle too?"

• • • ● • •

The people of Chelm were worriers. So they called a council meeting to do something about the problem. A motion was made that Yossel, the beggar, be retained by the community to do its worrying, and that his fee be one ruble per week. The motion was about carry when the wife of a local sage, Yenta, asked the fatal question: "Wait a minute. If Yossel earns a ruble a week, what would he have to worry about?"

And the Laughs Go On and On—Classics

Timeless we call them. Gems that are passed on from generation to generation because they are, simply—*classic*.

THE PORTRAIT

Mrs. Finkelstein is having her portrait done and conferring with the artist.

"Make my face so everyone will know it's me. Never mind pretty, just lifelike. Except, I want a pearl necklace, and in my hair a diamond tiara. Also, rubies hanging from my wrists and my ears."

"Okay," says the painter. "But it would be more realistic if you wore it."

"Are you crazy? I don't have jewelry like that. Make it up."

"But if you don't have jewelry, why do you want to be painted wearing it?"

"Because my husband took an oath he'll hang my portrait even after I die. And if that rat marries again, I want his floozy to go crazy trying to find it."

THE PHONE CALL

A hysterical young mother sprang to the ringing phone.

"So, darling, how are you?" said the voice.

"Rotten, Ma!" She sobbed. "The baby won't eat, the washer is leaking, so I slipped and sprained my ankle. Worse, company's coming and I can't shop because the car is broken!"

"Darling, stop crying. For you, I'll shop. Also, I'll send a repairman, twenty minutes tops. Then I'll feed the baby and make a brisket."

"Oh, Ma, . . . you're the best!"

"Please. What are mothers for? Listen, if the car's broken, how did Harold get to work?"

"Harold?"

"Harold! Your husband!"

"My husband's name is Norman."

"Norman? Is this 555-2122?"

"No. This is 555-2212." Then, after a pause, "Does this mean you're not coming?"

THE WILL

Goldstein has died. The family is listening to the reading of the will.

" '. . . and to my lovely wife, Sarah, who was there for me through even the ferocious button war of '52, I leave five million dollars. Enjoy, darling!"

Sarah wipes a tear.

"'And to my daughter Rachael, who, except for the ski bum, has been the light of my life . . . also five million!'"

More tears.

"'To my son David-the-lawyer, the same. Now get rid of the partner.'"

Louder oohs.

"'And finally . . . to my brother-in-law, Hymie, who lived with us ten years. Hymie, who wore my finest suits, smoked my best cigars, and didn't contribute a nickel. To Hymie, who said I'd never remember him in my will . . . 'Hello, Hymie!'"

PLOTNIK DIAMOND

Two middle-aged women are on an airplane bound for Miami. They have never met before.

"Excuse me," says the first woman "but I can't help noticing the diamond on your finger. Gorgeous."

"Thank you. It's forty carats," replies the other woman.

"Forty carats! I never heard from one so big!"

"I know. It even has a name."

"A name? So romantic! What's the name?"

"The Plotnik diamond. And believe me, it's not so romantic."

"Why?" asks the first woman.

"It comes with a terrible curse. Terrible!"

"Oy, pardon my asking, but what's the curse?"

"*Mister* Plotnik."

CHICKEN SOUP

During a performance in the Yiddish theater, the star keels over onstage. A doctor rushes to the stricken actor, when, from the balcony, there comes the voice of an old *bubbe* (granny).

"Give 'em some chicken soup. Give 'im some chicken soup!"

Ignoring her, the doctor continues laboring over the actor.

"Mistah—*Give 'im some chicken soup!*"

Finally, unable to ignore her any longer, the doctor looks toward the balcony.

"Madam," he says. "It wouldn't help."

"It vouldn't hurt."

Greats on Greats:
"The Lists" and Favorite Jokes

FREDDIE ROMAN

F reddie Roman is the comic's comic. In addition
to packing houses all over the country, he even
has a title! Dean. His institution? The Friars Club in
New York, with a flock that includes Buddy
Hackett, Alan King, Billy Crystal, Rob Reiner, and
Jerry Seinfeld. Born Fred Kirschenbaum in Newark,
New Jersey, Freddie, whose father "was in ladies'
shoes," got his start at a the Biltmore Hotel in the
Catskill Mountains. Management noticed the
young social director had potential (while he was
calling Simon Says and emceeing) and promoted
him to comic.

"I remember vividly driving past the Concord
Hotel in 1961, and I said to my wife, 'Someday I'm
going to star there on a Saturday night.' 'It would
be okay, if you're the opening act, too,' she said.
Nine years later he headlined at the Concord—for
thirty years, followed by twelve years at Caesars
Palace in Las Vegas. In 1991 he conceived and
costarred in the hit show *Catskills on Broadway* in
New York and then on tour.

Funniest Jewish Entertainers (Random Order)

Exclusive to *A Little Joy, A Little Oy*

Buddy Hackett	Totie Fields
Alan King	Walter Matthau
Shecky Greene	Myron Cohen
Jan Murray	Sam Levinson

MARTY ALLEN

How do you follow the Beatles' first appearance on *The Ed Sullivan Show*? If you're the comic legend Marty Allen, you introduce yourself as "Ringo's mother—then jump in the audience and go crazy." And the "Hello, Dere!" man with the Don King locks and eyes like neon Ping-Pong balls was still making crowds crazy with laughter performing with his beautiful wife and supertalented straight lady, the singer Karon Kate Blackwell, in Las Vegas. Following a successful solo career, "the love child of Phyllis Diller and Buddy Hackett," as Allen calls himself, hit the national comedy scene when Nat King Cole put him together with the singer Steve Rossi and the two became the biggest comedy hit duo since Martin and Lewis. Allen (born Alpern in Pittsburgh), (ex) door-to-door dance lesson salesman, Soldier's Medal recipient, tireless charity performer (particularly for Holocaust-related charities), actor, daytime TV star, art and book expert, *shmoozes* with his pals Sidney Sheldon and the Pulitzer Prize Winner John Toland.

If for a few moments I can make someone laugh, forget his pain, his disappointments, his unhappiness, well . . . that's the whole bag. That's what comedy and my performing are all about.

—MARTY ALLEN

Funniest Jewish Entertainers (Random Order)

Exclusive to *A Little Joy, A Little Oy*

Peter Sellers	Woody Allen
Jackie Mason	Shecky Greene
Buddy Hackett	Totie Fields
Mel Brooks	Ben Blue
Jerry Lewis	

Three booths next to us in the coffee shop in Las Vegas broke up when Marty told this joke.

A homeless guy knocks at the door and a Jewish woman answers: "*Nu?* What is it?"

"Lady, I'm homeless. I haven't eaten in three days."

"All right, would you eat yesterday's soup?" she asks.

"Yeah!"

"Okay. Come tomorrow!"

BERNIE ALLEN

Wherever people have laughed, Bernie Allen, born Bernard Kleinberg in 1916, has *been*—from the Copacabana in New York to the great hotels in the Catskills and Las Vegas. The World War II vet, former restaurant manager, and cabdriver got his big break when he picked up Rocky Graziano, who thought he was a riot and introduced him to Martha Raye. His career in stand-up was launched, and he went on to roles in films like *Raging Bull* and *The Producers*. On March 21, 2001, he was inducted into the Casino Legends Hall of Fame at the Tropicana Hotel in Las Vegas.

Favorite Jewish Entertainers (Random Order)

Exclusive to *A Little Joy, A Little Oy*	
Totie Fields	Shecky Greene
Red Buttons	Peter Sellers
Marty Allen	Jerry Seinfeld
Jan Murray	Phil Foster
Jack Carter	

Bernie Allen couldn't help but chuckle telling this one—accent-perfect:

A Jewish lady is sunning herself. It's 110 degrees. A pale, middle-aged man is walking toward her, dressed in a tie, shirt, and jacket.

She says, "Mister, come here a second. Take off the jacket, mit the tie and shoit, and go for a swim!"

"I can't. I'm just out of prison."

"For what?" she says.

"I killed my wife. I cut her up into little pieces and I stomped her into the ground."

She says (pause), "So . . . you're single?"

THE HILARIOUS HACKETTS: SANDY AND BUDDY

What career path do you choose when your father just happens to be "the funniest human being who ever walked the planet"? Meter reading is probably out. And Sandy Hackett, who made his own comedy mark headlining from Atlantic City to Las Vegas, can be seen and heard nationally on his syndicated *The Sandy Hackett Show.*

The New York City–born comedian says his legendary dad, Buddy Hackett (born Leonard Hacker), is not only the funniest man alive, but also the smartest. "When I was a kid I saved to buy an encyclopedia dictionary. When Dad saw it, he said, 'I think you're going to enjoy it.'" How did he know? He had read every word in it—and proved it to his then-young son!

Favorite Jewish Entertainers (Random Order)

Exclusive to *A Little Joy, A Little Oy*	
Shecky Greene	Freddie Roman
Jerry Lewis	Howie Mandel
Jack Benny	George Burns
Gilda Radner	Jerry Stiller
Elayne Boosler	And, of course, Buddy Hackett

Sandy gave a chuckle when he related one of his favorite Jewish lines: "The waiter who said to the table of Jewish women, 'Is *anything* okay?'"

You Don't Have to Be Jewish: Pat Cooper

"I ain't going away!" says Pat Cooper, the Brooklyn-born quintessential comic of Italian extraction who has been delighting audiences of all ethnicities for over forty years onstage, from Atlantic City to Las Vegas, and on TV with the likes of Carson, O'Brien, and Letterman.

When asked his all-time favorite Jewish joke, the venerable funnyman, who was honored on March 21, 2001, with an induction into the Casino Legends Hall of Fame at the Tropicana Hotel in Las Vegas, told the author the following without skipping a beat.

Jewish people eat more Italian food than the Italians.

Jewish people eat more Chinese than the Chinese.

They stopped eating—they close down two countries.

Favorite Jewish Entertainers (Random Order)

Exclusive to *A Little Joy, A Little Oy*	
Freddie Roman	Henny Youngman
Shecky Greene	Mickey Freeman
Jackie Mason	Dick Shawn

You Don't Have to Be Jewish: Pudgy!

Pudgy! The Queen of Tease, called a combination Totie Fields–Don Rickles, has played virtually every major room from New York to Atlantic City to Las Vegas with her unique improvisational style. In addition to headlining, Pudgy! shot a talk show for C1-TV.

Favorite Jewish Entertainers (Random Order)

Exclusive to *A Little Joy, A Little Oy*	
Jerry Lewis	Howie Mandel
Jackie Mason	Mal Z Lawrence
Totie Fields	Phyllis Diller
Don Rickles	Milton Berle
Mel Brooks	Jerry Seinfeld

OR MAYBE WHEN IT COMES TO HUMOR, THE WHOLE WORLD'S A LITTLE JEWISH?

Albert Einstein once said, "The Jewish religion . . . demands no act of faith—in the popular sense of the term—on the part of its members. And for that reason there has never been a conflict between our religious outlook and the world outlook of science." Which is perhaps why the science fiction legend Sir Arthur C. Clarke considers himself "an Honorary Jew."

His favorite Jewish joke?

Dear Marnie,

My favorite Jewish story:

"Mama—I've just won a Cadillac in the sweepstake!"
"Oy! You want to ruin us with gas bills?"

You're welcome to quote me. I've often called myself an Honorary Jew.

Love,

Arthur, June 17, Sri Lanka

Without Them,
WOULD THIS WORLD SOUND
OR LOOK SO LOVELY?

ARTUR SCHNABEL   Bette Midler
ITZHAK PERLMAN   BARBRA STREISAND
Isaac Stern   Beverly Sills   Leonard Bernstein
Benny Goodman   André Breton   Alan Jay Lerner
Richard Rodgers   Guggenheims
Marvin Hamlisch   Jule Styne
Oscar Hammerstein II   George Gershwin
IRA GERSHWIN   Jerome Kern   Marc Chagall
Irving Berlin   Artie Shaw   AARON COPLAND
CARLY SIMON   Herb Alpert   Sammy Cahn
Neil Diamond   NEIL SEDAKA   Stephen Sondheim
Yehudi Menuhin   Mel Tormé
Roberta Peters   Eddie Cantor   Steve Lawrence
Eydie Gormé   DINAH SHORE   PAUL SIMON
Melissa Manchester   ALFRED STIEGLITZ
Barry Manilow   Michael Feinstein
Sophie Tucker   Gene Simmons
Kurt Weill   Art Garfunkel   Robert Merrill
Richard Tucker   Jan Peerce
Arthur Murray   MAX ERNST   André Previn
Arthur Fiedler   Mama "Cass" Elliot
Nathan Milstein   CY COLEMAN

108

Artur Rubinstein   Al Hirschfeld
Robert Rauschenberg   Emil Gilels
Jerome Robbins   **VLADIMIR HOROWITZ**
Annie Leibovitz   Bock and Harnick   **James Levine**
GUS KAHN   *Alicia Markova*   Anna Pavlova
Fritz Kreisler   **David Oistrakh**   Mischa Elman
FRANK LOESSER   *Theodore Bikel*   Bruno Walter
Man Ray   Burt Bacharach   **Meyer Davis**
Oscar Levant   GEORGE M. COHAN
Percy Faith   Dave Brubeck
KANDER AND EBB   Jacques Offenbach
Billy Joel   *Ernest Bloch*   LARRY ADLER
JASCHA HEIFETZ   Camille Pissarro
Eugene Ormandy   Peter Yarrow
Morton Gould   Harold Arlen
ANDRÉ KOSTELANETZ   Amedeo Modigliani
Rube Goldberg   COMDEN AND GREEN
Jacques Lipchitz   *Jacob Epstein*   Franz Waxman
Randy Newman   ARNOLD SCHOENBERG   LIONEL BART
Arthur Schwartz   *Peter Max*
RICHARD AVEDON   CAROLE KING
Lorenz Hart   *STAN GETZ*   Paul Whiteman
Mark Rothko   *Buddy Rich*

*All have at least one Jewish parent.

On Coming to America

Kate (the mother): . . . My grandfather had to pick her [my grandmother] up to see the Statue of Liberty. This is what they dreamed of. Their whole life. To get to America. And when they saw that statue, they started to cry. The women were wailing, the men were shaking, everybody praying. You know why?

Eugene (the son): Because they were free.

Kate: Because they took one look at that statue and said, "That's not a Jewish woman. We're going to have problems again."

Eugene: That would be a riot. A Jewish Statue of Liberty. In her left hand, she'd be holding a baking pan . . . and in the right hand, held up high, the electric bill.

—NEIL SIMON'S *Broadway Bound*

Coming to America through Ellis Island was very similar to coming through the Red Sea. . . . You can't understand what it is to be a Jew today—you cannot understand it, unless you understand what it was to come through Ellis Island, to . . . the Golden Land. The Land that was . . . willing to let us to work and thrive. The land that was willing to separate religion from the state. Just enough to let religion thrive in our homes—and just enough to let the state protect everyone equally.

—RABBI MARC GELLMAN

HOLD THE BACK PAGE! THE *FORWARD*

For the Jewish immigrant, the task of bridging the Old and New Worlds was accomplished with the help of Abraham Cahan's Yiddish-language newspaper, the *Forward*. Liberal and pro-worker since its inception in New York City in 1897, the paper offered important information and great literature as well as practical advice, showcasing talents such as Isaac Bashevis Singer, who, in 1978, became the first Yiddish writer to win the Nobel Prize for literature; Elie Wiesel, another laureate; as well as Saul Bellow, Chaim Potok, Philip Roth, and Joseph Heller. In 1990 a *Forward* was launched in English, and in 1995 in Russian.

Since 1906, the *Forward* has also been the home of the "Bintel Brief" (a bundle of letters). Started by Cahan, the "Bintel Brief" had the important job of advising immigrants. From the start, the letters reflected their hard times and longings, along with questions of assimilation and changing values. Subjects included, for example, arguments among Jews from different parts of Europe, pointers on dealing with immigration officials, intermarriage, and, yes, how to deal with husbands who stayed out late (typical answer? Have them join lodges, unions, or educational circles) and women who served dry cookies at ladies' club meetings! (Don't make such a fuss.) All of which made the "Bintel Brief" not only important but one of the most entertaining and personal problem solvers in the world for those who often had nowhere else to turn. Desperate letters often began, "Worthy Editor" or "My dearest friends of the *Forward*."

FAR FROM THE HOMES THEY LEFT

By 1880, there were forty thousand Jews in the United States, mostly from Germany. In 1881, after intense Russian persecution under Alexander III, large numbers fled. By 1918, close to two million had arrived. Unlike others who came over as individuals, these Yiddish-speaking Jews fled as a *group*. With no home to return to, they were apt to settle in the United States. Regardless of challenges and often in crises, these uprooted families had to endure and survive in their new land.

My grandfather . . . had a cafe . . . but the czar closed all businesses of Jews so he came then [to America]. My mother came here . . . she was about thirteen, and my mother's family put him, my father, into the butcher business. And he named his butcher's shop "The Live and Let Live Meat Market" because it was right after World War I, and that was his personal protest, as well as his everyday philosophy.

—BELLA ABZUG,
the first Jewish woman elected to
Congress (from New York in 1970)

"What's moxie?" Arty, thirteen, asks Uncle
Louie while they're discussing Grandma:

Louie: " . . . No, I didn't like her, but I
respected her. Hell of a teacher, Ma was. . . .
She was no harder on us than she was on
herself. When she was twelve years old, her
old man takes her to a political rally in
Berlin. The cops broke it up. With sticks,
on horseback. . . . A cop bashes in her old
man's head, a horse goes down and
crushes Ma's foot. Nobody ever fixed it. It
hurts every day of her life but I never once
seen her take even an aspirin. . . . She
coulda had an operation but she used the
money she saved to get to this country
with her husband and six kids.

That's moxie, kid.

—NEIL SIMON'S *Lost in Yonkers*

It was only toward sleep that every wink of the eyelids could strike a spark . . . and kindle out of shadowy corners . . . such vivid jets of images—of the glint on tilted beards . . . of the dry light on grey stone stoops . . . of the glow on the outstretched, open palms of legions upon legions of hands hurtling toward him. . . .

It was only toward sleep one knew himself still lying on the cobbles, felt the cobbles under him, and over him, and scudding ever toward him like a black foam, the perpetual blur of shot and running feet, the broken shoes, new shoes, stubby, pointed, caked, polished, buniony, pavement-beveled, lumpish, under skirts, under trousers, shoes, over one and through one, and feel them all and feel, not pain, not terror, but strangest triumph. . . .

One might as well call it sleep."

—HENRY ROTH, *Call It Sleep*

• • • ● • • •

SAM KRICHINSKY, IN HIS EARLY TWENTIES,
WALKS ALONG A MAIN STREET IN BALTIMORE. . . .

"I came to America in 1914. . . . It was the
most beautiful place you've ever seen in your
life. . . . The sky exploded; . . . there were
fireworks. What a welcome it was. . . . I didn't
know where my brothers were. . . . I found a
man who knew the name Krichinsky. . . . I'll
never forget him. . . . He had such big shoes.
. . . This was how he made his living: . . . he
would break in shoes for the wealthy. . . .
I said, what a country this is! . . . Then we
arrived at this building. . . . A window opened
up, and my four brothers looked down and
saw me. . . . "Sam!"

  And that's when I came to America. It was
the Fourth of July.

—BARRY LEVINSON's film *Avalon*
(1990)

This Land Is Made for You and Me

New World, First Words

Beginning in 1478, under Ferdinand and Isabella, at least thirteen thousand secret Jews were executed. Yet the king and queen employed Jews, notably Don Isaac Abravanel (or Abarbanel) as finance minister, offering to make him an exception (he refused) when, on March 31, 1492, the Edict of Expulsion was signed. The last Jews left Spain on August 2, 1492, the day before Columbus sailed—also the day of mourning for the destruction of the First and Second Temples. Indeed, these are the words that open Columbus's journal: "So after having expelled the Jews from your dominions, Your Highnesses . . . ordered me to proceed," fueling speculation about Columbus's background.

Columbus's first expedition was financed by conversos (Jews forced to convert from 1391 to 1497 in Spain and Portugal who secretly practiced Judaism). His second voyage was also financed in part by valuables left by expelled Jews.

117

Columbus's Jews: Christopher Columbus's navigator, Luis de Torres, was Jewish. In 1492 he was also the first European to set foot on American soil. To escape the Inquisition, however, he was a *converso*—baptized the day before sailing. The first Jew to arrive in America who was *not* a convert (*converso*) was Jacob Barsimon (also found as Barsimson), a native of Holland, on August 22, 1654.

Other Jews who sailed with Columbus were Roderigo De Triana, a sailor (first to sight land); Maestre Bernal, physician-surgeon; Roderigo Sanchez De Segovia, Queen Isabella's inspector; Marco, a cook; and Alfonso De La Calle, a sailor.

HE MADE IT POSSIBLE

There would have been no Jews in the English Colonies if it had not been for the Messianic argument of the Dutch Rabbi Manasseh ben Israel (1604–1657). Since 1290 Jews had been banned in English lands. Rabbi Manasseh addressed Oliver Cromwell, insisting that England must allow Jews to settle on its soil or Judgment Day would never come for Christian or Jew, for "before all [prophesies] be fulfilled the people of G-d must first be dispersed into all the places and countries of the world." This coincided with Cromwell's desire to develop trade and commerce in the colonies. Eventually, Jews were allowed to settle in Britain and its colonies.

In 1627 Rabbi Manasseh started the first Hebrew press in Amsterdam, making it the center of Hebrew printing at the close of the seventeenth and throughout the eighteenth century.

While working his territory in the Great Lakes area in 1763, Chapman Abram, a Jewish trader, was captured during the siege of Detroit by Chief Pontiac (chief of the Ottaws). He was condemned to death. When tied to the stake, a thirsty Abram begged for a drink. When one of his captors offered a scalding hot broth, he threw it into the man's face. Awestruck, his captors saw this action as a sign of insanity, marking Abram as a special favorite of their Great Spirit. They released him immediately and returned his "merchandise"!

THE JEWISH PAUL REVERE OF THE SOUTH

"First Jew In South Carolina To Hold Public Office And To Die For American Independence" opens the inscription on a commemorative stone in honor of Francis Salvador, erected for the bicentennial celebration of the Jewish community of Charleston, 1950.

Salvador came to Charleston (Charles Town) from London in 1773 and served with distinction in the creation of his state and new nation. In 1775 he was the first Jew elected to public office as delegate to the first South Carolina Provincial Congress. A volunteer in an expedition against Indians and Tories, he was killed in an ambush near the Keowee River on August 1, 1776, becoming the first Jew to give his life in the Revolutionary War.

A JEWISH PATRIOT

Haym Salomon, a Polish-born Jew, was a major force in the American Revolution as a secret agent in British-occupied New York City. Then, after fleeing to Philadelphia in 1778 to escape arrest, he used his financial skills to help rescue the Continental government. A member of Mikveh Israel Congregation, he made the largest contribution toward its first building in 1782 and was a strong Jewish advocate, stating in print (1784): "I am a Jew; . . . I do not despair . . . that we shall obtain every . . . privilege . . . we aspire to enjoy along with our fellow-citizens." Yet, upon his death in 1785, he was technically bankrupt.

In Chicago there is a statue linking Washington, Salomon, and Robert Morris, with these words: "The government of the United States which gives to bigotry no sanction, to persecution no assistance."

OTHER "REVOLUTIONARY JEWS"

- Colonel Issac Franks: George Washington's right-hand man, in 1793 he provided his home in Germantown to Washington, bound for the Third Continental Congress in Philadelphia and sidetracked by the yellow fever epidemic. Franks became the first Jew to have his portrait painted by Gilbert Stuart.

- Dr. Philip Moses Russel was commended by Washington for serving as his surgeon during the harsh winter of 1777–78.

- Other famous Jewish combatants: Captain Richard Lushington, Lieutenant Colonel David S. Franks, Lieutenant Colonel Solomon Bush, and Ensign Mordecai Davis.

JEWS IN THE CIVIL WAR

Jewish Americans fought in this most tragic of wars on both sides of the battlefield, blue and gray.

- The banking firm of Seligman Brothers provided financial support to the Union Army.

- Judah Philip Benjamin served as both secretary of war and secretary of state for the Confederacy. The Confederate States of America had at least twenty-three Jewish American staff officers.

- Dr. David de Leon of South Carolina was the first surgeon general of the Confederacy. His counterpart for the Union was Dr. Jonathan Horowitz.

- When General Robert E. Lee surrendered to General Ulysses S. Grant on April 9, 1865, Benjamin B. Levy, one of six (some sources say seven) Jews awarded the Congressional Medal of Honor, was present.

When the greatest chiropodist in America meets the biggest, most important feet in America, what do you get? A perfect fit! This was the case between President Lincoln and Isachar Zacharie, a Jew who worked his way up, toe by toe, through Henry Clay, John C. Calhoun, and Secretary of War Edwin Stanton (who didn't buy his idea of chiropodists for each army regiment, but let him treat his feet). When Zacharie hit the top tootsies, the prez's praises made it into the *New York Herald*. The two became friends, and Zacharie took on other roles— as an undercover agent for Lincoln and peacemaker between North and South—supposedly involving the chiropodist's weird plan to conquer Mexico— which sent him back to feet. But his was an important "step" in establishing close ties between American leaders and Jews.

The Seixas,
A Family of *Menshen* (Good People)

In late August 1776, when news came that the British were approaching New York, the Rabbi of Congregation Shearith Israel, Gershom Mendes Seixas (1745–1816), closed the synagogue and safeguarded its ceremonial objects, displayed to this day. He was also the first native-born Jewish clergy in the United States, the first non-Episcopalian to serve as a trustee of Columbia University (1787–1815), and one of fourteen clergymen participating in George Washington's first inauguration (1787).

His brother, Benjamin Mendes (1748–1817), was one of the founders of the New York Stock Exchange, and his son, David, established the Deaf and Dumb Institute in Philadelphia and was among the first to discover efficient ways of burning anthracite coal.

And Another Brother, Moses . . .

"Sir:—Permit the children of the stock of Abraham to approach you with the most cordial affection. . . . We reflect on those days of . . . danger when the God of Israel, who delivered David from the peril of the sword, shielded your head in . . . battle; and we rejoice to think that the same spirit . . . rests and ever will rest upon you, enabling you to discharge the arduous duties of the Chief Magistrate of these States."

—MOSES SEIXAS,
Hebrew congregation of Newport,
Rhode Island, upon the visit of
President George Washington on
August 17, 1790.

George Washington, in a follow-up letter, wrote: "May the children of the stock of Abraham who dwell in this land continue to . . . enjoy the good will of the other inhabitants; while everyone shall sit in safety under his own vine and fig tree and there shall be none to make him afraid."

MORE AMERICAN PRESIDENTS ON JEWS

In addition to President Washington, others have stated their respect for Jews in America.

- John Adams: "I will consider that the Hebrews have done more to civilize man than any other nation."

- Benjamin Harrison: "The Hebrew is never a beggar; he has always kept the law—life by toil—often under severe and oppressive civil restrictions."

- Woodrow Wilson: "Here is a great body of our Jewish Citizens from whom have sprung men of genius in every walk of our varied life; men who have . . . led enterprises with spirit and sagacity. . . . They are not Jews in America, they are American citizens."

- Dwight Eisenhower: "I grew up believing that the Jews are the chosen people, that they gave us the high ethical and moral principles of our civilization."

- And . . . Benjamin Franklin contributed funds to lift the mortgage of one of the first synagogues in Philadelphia.

Yes, Jewish Americans, since the very start—and even before that—have played a key role in the founding and defending of the United States. Indeed, in times of strife and conflict, their military contributions have often exceeded their proportionate numbers.

SOME DATA . . .

During the Revolutionary War, there were approximately two thousand Jews in America. The vast majority of eligible males participated in the war; indeed, in South Carolina, because of the large number of Jews in the region, there was a primarily Jewish company.

• • • ◉ • •

About twenty thousand Jews fought in the Civil War, sharing the tragedy on both sides.

• • • ◉ • •

During the Spanish-American War, about five thousand Jewish Americans served, including thirty army officers and twenty naval officers.

In World War I, a quarter of a million American Jews served, representing more than their share of the population (5.73 percent in the armed forces versus 3.27 percent of the population). Over one thousand were decorated.

• • • ● • •

In World War II, once again, at over half a million, the proportion of Jewish Americans serving was larger than their percentage of the population (4.23 percent versus 3.33 percent). Fifty-two thousand were decorated.

• • • ● • •

About 150,000 Jewish Americans served during the Korean War; 30,000 in Vietnam, and 10,000 in the Gulf War.

• • • ● • •

On the Battlefields— and On All Fronts . . .

World War II, in body, in spirit, in image, was captured in perhaps the most famous and most photographed symbol of courage in battle. That is, of course, the United States Marines raising the flag atop Mount Suribachi on Iwo Jima. The photo, shot during combat, was taken by a Jew, Joe Rosenthal of the Associated Press, and he was awarded the Pulitzer Prize for this remarkable achievement.

Without Them, Would This World Be Quite So Prosperous?

Rothschilds   The Gimbels

THE FILENES   Helena Rubinstein

DAVID LUBIN—one of the earliest chain stores

Julius Rosenwald—oversaw Sears,

Roebuck & Co.   Calvin Klein

SYLVIA PORTER   MAX FACTOR

Donna Karan

HOWARD JONAS

Edgar Bronfman

ANDREW GROVE   Estee Lauder

LEVI STRAUSS

NICHOLAS PRITZKER—real estate

Ralph Lauren   Julia Waldbaum

Diane Von Fürstenberg

Charles Lazarus—Toys "R" Us

Ben & Jerry (Cohen and Greenfield)

ARTHUR BLANK AND BERNARD MARCUS—Home Depot

Armand Hammer

August Brentano

Isidor and Nathan Straus

The Levitts

André-Gustave Citroën

Ruth Handler—Barbie doll

Albert Lippert *Goldman Sachs*

Benjamin Altman *Louis Blaustein*

John Brunswick

IDA ROSENTHAL—Maidenform

MAX AND LEONARD STERN—Hartz Mountain

*All have at least one Jewish parent.

131

Famous
(and Not So Famous) Firsts

MASTER YIDDISH STORYTELLER:
ISAAC BASHEVIS SINGER

A master in] the tradition of such Yiddish story-telling masters as Medele, Peretz, Asch," wrote the *New York Times* on November 6, 1978, after Isaac Bashevis Singer became the first Yiddish-language writer to win the Nobel Prize in literature. Descended from Hassidic Rabbis, he was born in 1904 in Radzymin, Poland, and educated in Orthodoxy. Following his older brother, the writer Israel Joshua Singer (*The Family Carnowsky, The Brothers Ashkenazi*, epic Yiddish novels), to America in 1935, he worked for the *Jewish Daily Forward*, the New York Yiddish newspaper. With Saul Bellow's 1952 translation of "Gimpel the Fool," Singer's audience expanded. Many of his works, originally appearing in the *Forward*, were character-ized by sensuality and fablelike simplicity, garnering him a wider readership than perhaps any other Yiddish-language author. Isaac Bashevis Singer died on July 24, 1991, at age eighty-seven.

UNCOMMON MEN: THE ROTHSCHILDS

Lionel Nathan Rothschild (1808–1879), son of Nathan Mayer and grandson of the financier Mayer Amschel Rothschild (1744–1812), became the first Jewish member of the British House of Commons. But despite his election several times, he did not assume his seat for eleven years, until Parliament let him take the oath in a manner acceptable to the Jewish faith. Finally, on July 26, 1858, with head covered according to Jewish ritual, he took the oath on the Hebrew Bible. Lionel lived to see his son, Sir Nathan Mayer, the first Baron Rothschild (1840–1915), also a member of Parliament, become the first Jewish peer in Britain in 1855.

The Schwarzian is what the zeppelin should have been called, since the Austrian Jew David Schwarz invented the airship, building a proto-type in 1892. When the German government told him to proceed with production, he dropped dead from shock, which is how Count Zeppelin came to buy the patents from Mrs. Schwarz—and take the credit.

• • • ● • • •

HE SAW THE LIGHT:
ALBERT ABRAHAM MICHELSON

"The most important experiment that did not work in the whole history of science" was how the writer Isaac Asimov referred to the Michelson-Morley experiment in 1887 which used rays of light to determine the extent of the "ether"—and proved no such substance was floating around. The results were paradoxical. Evidently the speed of light plus any other added velocity was still equal only to the speed of light. To explain this, physics had to be recast, which resulted, eventually, in Albert Einstein's theory of relativity. So Michelson's work helped begin the tale of atomic research. The Prussian scientist, who came to America as a boy, accurately measured the speed of light, becoming the first American scientist to be awarded the Nobel Prize for physics in 1907.

ORVILLE AND WILBUR MOVE OVER:

The German Jew Otto Lilienthal made the first glider flights in Berlin in 1892 to develop theories of aerodynamics. He was considering a motor, when, on August 10, 1896, he lost control in a sudden wind and fell to his death. An inspiration to the Wright Brothers, according to *The American Heritage History of Flight,* Lilienthal was the first to demonstrate "air could support a man in winged flight."

A BARRIER BROKEN: SALLY PRIESAND

In 1972, Sally Priesand was ordained as the first female American Rabbi. Of the occasion, she said, "Even in Reform Judaism, [women] were not permitted to participate fully in the life of the synagogue. With my ordination all that was going to change; one more barrier was about to be broken. . . . I decided to do this so that I would be the first woman rabbi to carry a torch for the feminist movement."

Forget the earl of Sandwich. The great Jewish teacher Hillel (60 B.C.E.–9 C.E.) made the first sandwich by placing bitter herbs between two pieces of matzah for a Passover Seder—a tradition still followed today.

A MEDICAL GROUNDBREAKER: ROSALYN SUSSMAN YALOW

Rosalyn Sussman Yalow, the daughter of German and American Jews, neither of whom completed high school, received her degree from Hunter College in physics and chemistry. Rejected from Purdue's graduate program because of both her gender and her religion, she got her Ph.D. in nuclear physics (1945) from the University of Illinois, becoming the first woman in their College of Engineering. At the VA Hospital in 1947, she and her partner, Dr. Solomon A. Berson, created radioimmunoassay (RIA), allowing doctors to diagnose conditions caused by minute changes in hormone levels, useful in diabetes, screening for hepatitis in blood banks, determining effective dosages of antibiotics, and more in the field of endocrinology. Among her many honors she was the first American woman to win the Nobel Prize in medicine and physiology in 1977.

• • • ● • •

Marconi invented the radio, but it was Heinrich Rudolph Hertz who caught the "big wave"—radio waves—and how to generate, transmit, and detect them (1887–1889).

Rabbi Levi ben Gershon (1288–1344) invented Jacob's staff, the nautical instrument that enabled sailors in the Middle Ages to figure out (okay, chart) where they were. His thinking also laid the groundwork for modern trigonometry.

• • • ● • • •

JEWISH JEANS: LEVI STRAUSS

That quintessentially American item, denim blue jeans, was the work of Levi Strauss, a Bavarian immigrant born in 1829. Lured west by the Gold Rush, he sailed to San Francisco in 1850 loaded with canvas for tents and wagons. But he found a better use for the material—overalls for miners. Later he switched to denim. After a Nevada tailor riveted the pocket corners for strength, they got a patent in 1873—and blue jeans ("riveted-waist overalls") were born! During World War II, Levi's were declared an essential commodity, limited to those in defense work. In 1935 jeans became fashionable when they were featured in *Vogue*. Designer jeans became so hot that in the seventies, they were virtually an underground unit of currency in Communist countries. In 1997 Levi Strauss & Co. paid a dealer $25,000 for a pair of Levi's 501 jeans, circa 1890–1901.

• • • ● • • •

PLAY IT AGAIN, EMILE

The phonograph was the brainchild not of Thomas Edison but of Emile Berliner, who invented the gramophone. And he made a fortune selling records and players, and opening the first recording studio (1897). The forerunner of RCA absorbed his company, and the famous logo—the dog listening to "his master's voice."

The first semi-talkie motion picture, *The Jazz Singer* (1927), with musical numbers in sound was a Jewish creation in production (Warner Bros.), in star (Al Jolson), and in topic. The Lithuanian-born Jolson (born Asa Yoelson), whose hits included "April Showers," "Toot Toot Tootsie," "California, Here I Come," "Rockabye Your Baby," was the son of a cantor and played the son of a cantor.

• • • ● • • •

MATZAH, MATZAH MAN!

In the 1880s Cincinnati wasn't teeming with Kosher ready-made foods. But this was a problem that Rabbi Dov Behr Manischewitz solved by starting a small matzah bakery in 1888. Instead of using black-iron coal stoves, he used new gas-fired ovens, giving him more control over the baking. His reputation as a baker grew beyond Cincinnati—and the rest became delicious history as three generations expanded and diversified, making the Manischewitz name synonymous with Kosher wine and other Kosher products. Today the company is the nation's largest manufacturer of processed Kosher foods and the world's number-one baker of matzah.

In 1861, fifteen years before Alexander Graham Bell patented his device, Johann Philipp Reis, a German Jew, exhibited his telephone to scientists in Europe, where he transmitted a song over a three-hundred-foot line to a hospital.

• • • ● • • •

THE APOSTLE OF BATHING TO
THE APOSTLE OF PRESIDENTS

An advocate of cleanliness as preventive medicine, Dr. Simon Baruch (1840–1921), a Prussian-Polish immigrant who served in the Confederacy as a surgeon, moved to New York City and opened America's first public bath. More, in 1888 he was the first doctor to diagnose the need for, then perform, an appendectomy. Relatively speaking, the good doctor went on to father yet another "apostle"—in the political arena—Bernard Baruch, adviser to presidents.

A HEARTBEAT AWAY: JOSEPH LIEBERMAN

> Part of [my involvement in politics] has to do with my Jewish education and the whole tradition in Judaism of an obligation to try to do justice, to try to better the community, and to try to make a difference.
>
> —JOSEPH LIEBERMAN

When Senator Joseph Lieberman, a devout Jew, took the podium at the Democratic Convention in Los Angeles on August 16, 2000, after having been chosen as Vice President Al Gore's running mate, there was scarcely a Jew, regardless of political party, who wasn't *kvelling* (beaming with pride). This was most particularly true in Lieberman's own congregation,

Westville Beth Hamedrosh Hagodol B'nai Israel, in Connecticut. For, by accepting the candidacy, Lieberman, the son of working-class parents, became the first Jew to run for national office. In the closest presidential race in history, after weeks of legal disputes in Florida, that state's twenty-five electors were assigned to the opposition on December 12, giving the Republicans the presidency.

FAMOUS U.S. JEWISH FIRSTS: QUICKIES

Admiral: Adolph Marix, advanced to rear admiral by President Taft, July 4, 1908

Ambassador: Oscar Solomon Straus, to Ottoman Turkey, March 24, 1887. He was also the first Jewish Cabinet member, of Commerce and Labor in 1906.

Army chaplain (ordained): Rabbi Jacob Frankel, September 10, 1862

Bat Mitzvah: Judith Kaplan, 1922

College (Jewish): Maimonides College, Philadelphia, October 28, 1867

Congressional representative: Israel Jacobs, Second Congress, March 4, 1791–March 3, 1793

Congresswoman: Bella Abzug, 1970

Doctor trained in America: Isaac Abraham, 1774

Hebrew book (all): Abne Yehoshua (Stones of Joshua), published 1860 in New York City

Hebrew grammar book: Published 1735 in Boston for use at Harvard College

Kosher butcher: Asser Levy, Brooklyn, 1660

Lawyer: Moses Levy qualified/admitted to the Pennsylvania bar in 1778

Medal of Honor: Sergeant Leopold Karpeles, Battle of the Wilderness, May 1864, issued April 30, 1870

Miss America: Bess Myerson, 1945

Navy captain: Uriah P. Levy, served in the War of 1812, advanced March 1844

Naval chaplain: Rabbi David Goldberg, appointed lieutenant junior grade, October 30, 1917

Postage stamp: Samuel Gompers on a three-cent stamp issued January 27, 1950

Prayer book: Published 1766 by John Holt in New York

Pulitzer Prize for reporting: Herbert Bayard Swope (*New York World*), June 4, 1917

Rabbi to lead the opening prayer for a session of Congress: Rabbi Morris Raphael, 1860

Rabbinical school: Hebrew Union College, founded by Rabbi Isaac M. Wise, 1875

Reform Judaism: Established 1854 by Rabbi Isaac M. Wise in Cincinnati

Secretary of State: Henry Kissinger, 1973

U.S. Senator: David Levy Yulee, from Florida, elected July 1, 1845

Supreme Court Justice: Louis D. Brandeis, appointed by President Wilson, sworn in June 3, 1916.

Supreme Court Justice (woman): Ruth Bader Ginsburg, sworn in August 10, 1993

Veterans' organization: Hebrew Union (forerunner to the Jewish War Veterans of the United States of America, which is recognized as the oldest veterans' organization in America) March 15, 1896

West Point graduate: Simon M. Levy, October 12, 1802

West Point graduate (woman): Donna Maller, June 4, 1980

Without Them,
WOULD THIS WORLD BE
QUITE AS ADVANCED?

ALBERT EINSTEIN   **Judith Resnik**—astronaut

Heinrich Hertz—electronics   **Konrad Block**—physics

Béla Schick—diphtheria test

ROSALYN SUSSMAN YALOW—medicine

LILLIAN D. WALD—visiting nurses

Isaac Hayes—AMA   **JONAS SALK**

Felix Block—physics

ALBERT ABRAHAM MICHELSON—physics

Carl Sagan   **Michael Brown**—physiology

Donald Glaser—physics   Edwin Land

Landsteiner, Levine and Weiner—blood   **Albert Sabin**

Steven Weinberg—physics

J. ROBERT OPPENHEIMER

SIGMUND FREUD   **ARTHUR KORNBERG**—DNA

Lise Meitner—physics

JULIAN SCHWINGER—electrodynamics

NIELS BOHR—physics

Baruch Blumberg—physiology

Donald Blazer—physics

Murray Gel-Mann—physics   **Erich Fromm**

Edward Teller—physics   John von Neumann—math

Otto Lilienthal—aerodynamics

Selman Abraham Waksman—streptomycin

Salvador Luria—medicine, physiology

Joseph Goldberger—nutrition

William Herschel and Caroline Lucretia
Herschel—astronomy   Casimir Funk—vitamins

Nathan Strauss—pasteurization in the United States

Norbert Wiener—math/cybernetics

Simon Baruch—appendectomy/public baths

Abraham Jacobi—father of American pediatrics

PAUL EHRLICH—syphilis cure

August von Wassermann—syphilis test

Harold Varmus—medicine

GREGORY GOODWIN PINCUS—medicine

George Dantzig—math

GERTRUDE B. ELION—medicine

Stephen Jay Gould—paleontology

Leon M. Lederman—physics

*All have at least one Jewish parent.

145

It's the *Emmes* (Truth)!

"Mr. and Mrs. Cohen are pleased to announce the birth of their son—Dr. Cohen."

Okay, it's true. All those Jewish doctor jokes have a basis.

The Talmud makes reference to anesthesia, amputations, false teeth, artificial limbs, and even contraception. During the Middle Ages about half of all Jewish intellectuals were doctors. One such was Amatus Lusitanus, physician to Pope Julius III in the 1500s.

· · · ● · ·

Moses Maimonides (1135–1204), the greatest rabbinic thinker and physician of his time, was personal physician to the Sultan Saladin. His treatises on asthma, poisons, hemorrhoids, and sex were studied in universities for five centuries following his death.

· · · ● · ·

The first U.S. pediatrician was Dr. Abraham Jacobi (1830–1919), who treated, taught, and created clinics.

DID YOU TAKE YOUR A–ZINC TODAY?

If so, it is because Casimir Funk, a Polish Jew, who came to the United Stats in 1915, discovered that a compound from yeast proved powerful in curing beriberi. Thinking it belonged to a class called amines (nitrogen), he termed his discovery *vitamine* (*vita* meaning "life"). He further put forth the notion that other diseases, such as scurvy and rickets, came from similar "vitamine" deficiencies. His theory was incorrect only insofar as not all "vitamines" were amines. In 1920, the British scientist Cecil Drummond labeled certain substances that were soluble using Funk's term, but dropping the *e* to omit the concept of amines. *It's the Emmes!*

A LITTLE VINEGAR ON YOUR BURGER?

If your response is "yechh," you have one Dr. Siccary, a Portuguese Jew, who became a pioneer physician in Virginia, to thank. For it was the good doctor who, in 1733, explained that the plant, known as the love apple was in fact not poisonous and was more useful than a mere a garden ornament. Indeed, it was healthful and edible. That plant was the tomato!

AND SPEAKING OF FOOD . . .
IS THE MOON CREAM CHEESE?

The king of Jewish food, the bagel, has become universal, but who knew how universal? An article in the October 1999 issue of *Moment* magazine reported that scientists are beginning to wonder if the universe is bagel-shaped.

"It's a serious cosmological question," said Tony Rothman, professor at Illinois Wesleyan University, in the article. "The popular notion is that the universe is expanding spherically." But, said Dr. Rothman in a follow-up call with the author, "some scientists believe that the expanding universe may indeed be shaped like a bagel," a hypothesis that is discussed in detail in his book, *Doubt and Certainty* (Perseus, 1998). Ah, but if it's true we have new questions to answer, such as "whether the universe is onion or sesame seed," quipped the professor.

A VULCAN SALUTE

Leonard Nimoy, the Jewish actor, noted for playing Spock on *Star Trek*, was reportedly the inspiration behind the character's live-long-and-prosper greeting. The five fingers held upright and split between middle and ring fingers is a gesture used by the Jewish High Priest (the Kohen).

BY AN EMPEROR, HE'S NO EMPEROR

Most people know we have a president, but for a brief shining twenty years, we also had an emperor. A Jewish one yet. Norton the First.

Joshua Abraham Norton, a London-born Jew, arrived in San Francisco in 1849 and did very well selling mining supplies. But, after failing to corner the rice market, he lost everything, disappeared, then reappeared at the offices of the *San Francisco Bulletin,* in seedy navy regalia and beaver hat, proclaiming himself "Emperor of these United States." The amused editor published the story in 1859, thus beginning the reign of Norton. He was a beloved figure over the years; San Franciscans bowed and curtsied as Norton sailed through the streets ensuring order. He was a welcome guest at every public function, his "endorsements" gave him free entree to restaurants, and the city paid for his lodging and uniforms. More, his "edicts" sparked slow news days. Here are a few examples.

December 2, 1859: Norton I dismissed Governor Wise of Virginia for hanging John Brown.

July 16, 1860: Norton I dissolved the United States of America.

October 1, 1860: Norton I barred Congress from meeting in Washington, D.C.

On January 8, 1880, he died of apoplexy on his way to a lecture. The headline the next day in the *Morning Call* read: "Norton the First, by the grace of God Emperor of the United States and Protector of Mexico, departed this life." *It's the Emmes!*

HE PLAYED THE HORSES, BIG TIME

The Belmont Stakes, one of the legs of the Triple Crown, and the track Belmont Park were named for a Jew, the German-born August Schonberg, who became a leading American financier and, in 1860, chairman of the Democratic National Committee. Why Belmont instead of Schonberg? *Both* mean "beautiful mountain." August translated the German to French!

WEST TO EAST—THE FLYING KOSHER PIZZA

Our story starts at the famed Broadway's Jerusalem 2, home of New York City Flying Pizzas. The owner, Eddie Fishbaum, and his brother Ari, received a fax from one Eiji Bando, with the plea "I'm hungry! Please deliver No. 1 pizza!" To Japan! In person! True to their vow to "deliver anywhere," valiant Eddie, yarmulke (skullcap) in place, delivered. And earned a place in Guinness World Records 2001, traveling 6,914 miles to hand over the Kosher pizza to Bando, a sports and media star, on April 1, 1998. The feat cost seven thousand dollars and was shown on Japanese TV. Never one to shirk research, the author called the Flying Pizzas in New York, and they delivered (okay, not in person) to Nevada. Now, if you'll excuse . . . oops . . . there's a crumb . . . mmmm, oy . . . sooo good . . .

· · ● · ·

THE JEWISH KING?

Along with David and Solomon, Jews can also lay (some) claim to the hipp-i-est king of all, Elvis! His maternal great-great-grandmother, Nancy Tackett, was Jewish. According to traditional Jewish law, religious identity passes through the mother, and the line between Tackett and Elvis is female, so . . .

Elvis could be considered a Jew! *It's the Emmes!*

HE SPREAD THE WORD

The Reuter's News Agency, the European counter-part of the Associated Press and United Press International, was founded by Paul Julius Reuter (born Israel Beer Josaphat), a German Jew. But did you know that the former bank clerk launched his illustrious career dispatching the news with homing pigeons? In 1849 he started a pigeon post service to bridge a gap in the telegraph line between Aachen, Germany, and Verviers, Belgium. However, he utilized more sophisticated methods when in 1851 he moved to England, became a citizen, and opened his news agency. The agency boomed, particularly after relaying an 1858 speech by Napoleon III. In 1871, the duke of Saxe-Coburg-Gotha made Reuter the Baron Paul Julius von Reuter.

FROM *TITANIC* TO TV

Most of us connect the name David Sarnoff with broadcasting. But the Russian-born Jew, who had the idea of radios that could "bring music into homes by wireless," was made a brigadier general by President Roosevelt and dubbed Father of American Television by the Television Broadcasters Association. What many may *not* know is that it was this same Sarnoff who, at age twenty-one, following the *Titanic* disaster on April 14, 1912, remained glued to his wireless earphones for seventy-two hours in the telegraph station at John Wanamaker's New York store and was one of the first to relay the names of the survivors to the world.

ON ACCOUNT OF A CART

Jews have always loved shopping—almost as much as talking. And eating. And making jokes, which brings me to Sylvan Goldman. Who, you may ask, is Sylvan Goldman? The man who invented the single most important object in retail. Sylvan Goldman, a Humpty Dumpty store owner in Oklahoma City, converted folding chairs, mounted them on wheels, and introduced the first viable shopping cart, in 1937.

That very cart is on display at the State Museum of Oklahoma, in Oklahoma City. *It's the Emmes!*

MY SON THE GENIUS

This phrase was probably not on the lips of Hyman and Rebecca when, in 1884, their seven-year-old, Joshua Lionel Cowen (born Cohen), attached a small steam engine to a wooden locomotive—and blew up the wallpaper. As a teen, however, he invented an electric doorbell, then dropped the idea when his teacher at Peter Cooper Institute called it impractical. Worse, he lost a fortune selling rights to his electric flowerpot. True, it wasn't a hit. But when the buyer detached the tubes and marketed the Eveready flashlight . . . oy. Finally, with a friend, Joshua launched the Lionel Manufacturing Co. in 1900. After an attempt to sell a portable electric fan, he again turned to his boyhood fascination and attached the fan's motor to a miniature wooden railroad car. This time it didn't explode. It moved. He was a genius after all, and Lionel trains were born.

TALK ABOUT YOUR ABSENTEE BALLOTS!

David Wolf worked as a doctor for the air force before becoming an astronaut in 1990. He has logged over three thousand hours in space, first, in 1993, flying aboard *STS-58*, where he spent fourteen days studying the effects of microgravity on the body. In 1997, while at the *Mir* space station to study life sciences, he became the first American to cast a vote from outer space! (Better *Mir* than Miami!)

And while we're in the atmosphere . . . The astronaut Jeffrey Hoffman, who flew on the space shuttles *Discovery* and *Columbia,* took Judaic objects with him on each flight. He brought the Torah aboard *Columbia. It's the Emmes!*

OY, HAVE I GOT GAS!

Petroleum was discovered not by an Arab or a Texan but by an Austrian Jew named Abraham Shreiner, an amateur scientist who found one could use the substance for lighting. In 1853, a year before the Americans "discovered" the process, he built a distillation plant. More, one Louis Blaustein and his son Jacob, from Maryland, were among the first to create the drive-in gas station by developing a pump that registered for the customer how much he was getting for his nickel. Wait, it gets better! The Blausteins developed the first antiknock gasoline, called Amoco (American Oil Company)—the fuel used by Charles Lindbergh on his historic flight from New York to Paris in the *Spirit of St. Louis* in 1927.

• • • ● • • •

THE "JEWISH" POPE

Anacletus II, elected Pope in 1130, was the great-grandson of Baruch, a Jewish businessman in Rome. When Pope Benedict IX told Baruch, an adviser, he would have to convert in order to maintain their ties, Baruch agreed officially—yet still practiced Judaism. This papal connection was passed on to Baruch's son, then to his grandson, who took the name Pierleonie. Finally, Baruch's great-grandson Pietro became a Catholic cleric, working his way up to cardinal. In 1130, Pietro Pierleonie, taking the name Anacletus II, was elected Pope—but not without great controversy and rivalry, with one Innocent II also elected, albeit by a smaller number of cardinals. The debates grew so fierce that each excommunicated the other. Nevertheless, Anacletus II—descended from the Jewish Baruch—remained Pope until his death in 1138, though he is considered an antipope in papal history, given the double election. *It's the Emmes!*

VIPs

Way before the establishment of the State of Israel in 1948, Jews were heads of governments across three continents. *It's the Emmes!*

Match the leaders with the places.

Country	Leader
1. France	A. Sir Isaac Isaacs
2. Italy	B. Luigi Luzzatti
3. England	C. Béla Kun
4. Australia	D. Benjamin Disraeli*
5. Bavaria	E. Léon Blum
6. Austria	F. Kurt Eisner
7. Hungary	G. Pierre Mèndes-France
8. India	H. Sidney Sonnino
9. Palestine	I. Bruno Kreisky
	J. Sir Herbert Samuel
	K. Marquis of Reading
	L. Rene Mayer

*Born and reared as a Jew until age twelve, then was baptized in the Church of England. However, Disraeli never denied his heritage.

1—E; G; L; 2—B; H; 3—D; 4—A; 5—F; 6—I; 7—C; 8—K; 9—J

FOR YOU TRIVIA BUFFS, A FEW QUICKIES.
IT'S THE *EMMES!*

"The Bridge that couldn't be built" was. By Joseph Strauss, a brilliant Jewish engineer who designed San Francisco's Golden Gate Bridge. It was opened to pedestrian traffic in 1937.

• • • • • •

Most know that Robert Briscoe, a Jew, was lord mayor of Dublin, but few know that *Rome* also had a Jewish mayor, from 1907 to 1913, whose name was Ernesto Nathan.

• • • • • •

The Lincoln head penny was designed by a Russian Jewish immigrant, Victor David Brenner, in 1909 to celebrate Lincoln's hundredth birthday.

• • • • • •

Was the old song "Did Your Mother Come from Ireland?" composed by an O'Brien, a Fitzgerald, a McDonald? Nope! The song was written by the Dublin-reared Michael Carr, born Cohen.

WANDER ENOUGH AND SOMETHING INTERESTING IS BOUND TO HAPPEN

Charlemagne appointed a Jew (Isaac) as interpreter and guide for an embassy to be established in Baghdad. Isaac returned in 802, causing quite a *mishegoss* (craziness) when he brought back a gift from the caliph to the emperor never before seen in the West—an elephant!

• • • ● • •

Years after the Colossus of Rhodes, one of the Seven Wonders of the World, was destroyed by an earthquake, guess who picked up the pieces? A Jew purchased the debris and shlepped it away on nine hundred camels.

It's the Emmes!

For You Sports Fans
(Okay, *Fan*) Out There

We have all heard the old joke that the thinnest book on record must be Jewish sports heroes, but there have been many superb Jews in athletics.

BALL (AND BOYCHICK) ONE!

The very first pro baseball player was none other than a Jew, Lipman Pike. "Lip" accepted twenty dollars a week to play third base for the Philadelphia Athletics in 1866, and soon other top players followed his lead. Within three years Cincinnati became the first all professional baseball team. Not only was Pike the first pro player, but he was baseball's first home run champion! The precise number is unknown, but we do know he hit six homers in one game in July 1866. Primarily an outfielder, Pike, a southpaw, played all positions during his nearly twenty-year career and managed numerous teams, including the Brooklyn Atlantics, Philadelphia Athletics, Cincinnati Red Stockings, and the original New York Mets. Pike died in 1893.

Wait, it gets better . . .

THE WORLD SERIES WAS A JEWISH CREATION!

Barney Dreyfuss, a German Jew, owned the Pittsburgh Pirates from 1900 to 1932 and built the first modern steel-frame triple-tier stadium, Forbes Field, in 1909. Dreyfuss challenged the American League champions, the Boston Pilgrims (later the Red Sox), to a postseason tournament. His team lost in a 5–3 upset, but when the first game was played, October 1, 1903, the World Series was born! During Dreyfuss's thirty-two-year reign as president and general manager, Pittsburgh finished in the first division twenty-six times, winning six pennants—1901, 1902, 1903, 1909, 1925, 1927— and the World Series in 1909 and 1925!

MVP

Al "Flip" Rosen, the South Carolina–born Jewish third baseman for the Cleveland Indians, made history when he was major league baseball's first unanimous selection as Most Valuable Player, in 1953. Rosen drove in a hundred or more runs from 1950 to 1954, led the American League in RBI's in 1952 and 1953, was the league's home run champion twice, led the league in total bases and, in 1953, in slugging percentage. Persistent injuries forced Rosen, born on March 1, 1925, into premature retirement following the 1956 season.

> We shall miss him on the infield
> and shall miss him at the bat,
> but he's true to his religion—
> and I honor him for that.
>
> —EDGAR GUEST, 1934

These are the last lines of a poem written in honor of "Hammer'n Hank" Greenberg when the baseball great who led the Detroit Tigers to win their first American League pennant refused to play on Yom Kippur in 1934. In 1938, with fifty-eight home runs, he almost beat Babe Ruth's record of sixty but set a major league mark when he slammed two homers per game eleven times. After his discharge from the army in June 1945, Hank hit a home run for the Tigers in his first game back and blasted his famous grand slam home run in the last inning of the final game of the season. The man Joe DiMaggio called "one of the truly great hitters," Henry Benjamin Greenberg, born in New York in 1911, was the first Jew elected to the Baseball Hall of Fame, in 1956.

• • • ● • • •

The Jewish kid is probably the best of them, said Casey Stengel in answer to the question "Who was the finest pitcher in baseball history?"

Casey was referring to Sandy Koufax. Although the L.A. Dodger southpaw pitching star played on the Sabbath when scheduled, like Greenberg before him he would not appear in the first game of the World Series against the Minnesota Twins because it fell on Yom Kippur in 1965. Instead, he went to synagogue and fasted. His father, who thought baseball "a stupid game," was nevertheless proud of his son's famous decision, calling him "a good Jewish boy."

The first All-Jewish basketball team—the South Philadelphia Hebrew Association (American Basketball League)—was founded by Eddie Gottlieb in 1918. SPHAS was written in Hebrew on their uniforms. The team bit the dust in 1949.

The world-famous Harlem Globetrotters was founded in Chicago by the London-born Jew Abe Saperstein, on January 7, 1927.

• • • ● • • •

THE (SEMI) ULTIMATE JEWISH SPORTS QUIZ

1. Joe Jacobs	A. Seventies Yankee slugger; the Kosher Bomber
2. Larry Sherry	B. Pitcher for the Dodgers in '59 World Series
3. Sid Luckman	C. Announcer; started as a lawyer; died in 1995
4. Ron Bloomberg	D. Chicago Bears quarterback; led team to four NFL championships in the '40s
5. Joey Cornblitt	E. Jai alai player
6. Howard Cosell	F. "Yussel the Muscle," Schmeling's manager: "We wuz robbed."
7. Allie Sherman	G. Light and welterweight champion in the '30s
8. Battling Levinsky	H. Olympic gold for Britain in track (1924); immortalized in *Chariots of Fire* (1981)

9. Lillian Copeland	I. Coach, New York Giants, 1961–69
10. Dick Savitt	J. Four Olympic swimming gold medals in 1968 and seven in '72
11. Nat Fleischer	K. Gold medal, 1932 Olympics, discus
12. Barney Ross	L. Coach–general manager, Boston Celtics, 1950–84
13. Mark Spitz	M. 1951 Wimbledon champ
14. Harold Abrahams	N. Light heavyweight champ 1979; the Jewish Bomber; wore Star of David on trunks
15. "Red" Auerbach	O. Light heavyweight champ, 1916–20
16. Mike Rossman	P. Fifties boxing writer

1–F; 2–B; 3–D; 4–A; 5–E; 6–C;
7–I; 8–O; 9–K; 10–M; 11–P; 12–G;
13–J; 14–H; 15–L; 16–N

HOOP SKIRTS

Senda Berenson, a Lithuanian Jew, became a legend in basketball history when, after being named the first director of physical education at Smith College in 1892–just one month after basketball had been invented by James Naismith—she organized the first women's collegiate basketball game at Smith. Influenced by the thinking of her time about women's physical limitations, she soon adapted the rules to avoid the roughness of the men's game. In 1891 she became editor of A. G. Spalding's first *Women's Basketball Guide,* further spreading her version of basketball for women. Berenson was one of the first two women (along with Margaret Wade) elected to the Basketball Hall of Fame in 1984.

MOTHER OF WOMEN'S SWIMMING

From a New York court stenographer who wanted some exercise after work, Charlotte Epstein (1884–1938) went on to become a modern Olympic pioneer in women's swimming. After forming the Women's Swimming Association to promote the health benefits of the sport, she guided many women to Olympic victory and was the U.S. Women's Olympic Swimming Team's manager throughout the twenties. Under her leadership, fifty-one world records were set.

The next time you hit a strike, think of John M. Brunswick—his name is all over his bowling and billiard equipment. The Jewish entrepreneur founded the Brunswick Corporation.

THE STRONGEST MAN IN THE WORLD

The first featherweight to lift more than eight hundred pounds and to press double his body weight was a cantor and son of a Rabbi! Isaac "Ike" Berger, who was born in Jerusalem in 1936 and came to America in 1955, won numerous national titles and was an Olympic champion. He took home the gold in 1956 with a lift of 776.5 pounds and the silver in 1960 and '64. In '64, he also set an Olympic record of 336 pounds in the clean and jerk at a body weight of 130, which made him the strongest man in the world. He held this record for nine years.

CATCHER-SPY

The mysterious Morris Berg was a Princeton and Columbia Law School graduate, a linguist, a not-too-terrific catcher with the Brooklyn Dodgers, Chicago White Sox, Cleveland Indians, Washington Senators, and Boston Red Sox (1923–1936)—and a spy during World War II. Berg, the son of Russian Jews (his father felt his son's first career choice was a waste), left the game on January 14, 1942, the day his father died. Fluent in Japanese and German (among many other languages), he became an officer in the Office of Strategic Services (the forerunner of the CIA) in 1943 and was assigned overseas, where he was involved in assessing how to deal with Werner Heisenberg, head of Nazi Germany's atom-bomb project. When Berg died at the age of seventy on May 19, 1972, his ashes were taken to Israel.

THE ORIGINAL SCREWBALL

Al Schacht, a pitcher for the Newark Bears, spent so much time joking rather than throwing that by 1914 he was often tossed out of games. In 1919, after joining the Washington Senators, he and a coach of the Senators, Nick Altrock, began entertaining fans with screwball skits (balls bouncing off their heads) before and between games, and they brought the house down at the 1922 World Series with a take-off on Rudolph Valentino. In 1933 Schacht went solo, and in 1936 he turned his full attention to the shtick, performing in virtually every ballpark until 1968.

Sidney Franklin, a Jewish boy from Brooklyn, did something no other Jewish boy from Brooklyn (or probably anywhere) ever did. In fact only a handful of U.S. citizens ever did. He went to Mexico and Spain and became a successful bullfighter, rising from *novillero* (apprentice) to *matador de toros* in 1932!

Sidney Franklin wasn't the only Jewish athlete who favored "exotic sports." Here is a small sampling:

Polo: Since the 1890s, members of the Rothschild family helped popularize the posh game in Austria and France. Other famous players included Adam Gimbel and John Schiff.

Roller Skating: The first singles skater to win the World Free Championship four times was Scott Cohen, in 1985, 1986, 1989, and 1990.

Rowing: Sir Archibald Levin Smith helped the Cambridge crew team defeat Oxford in the Henley Royal Regatta in 1858. The Lone Star Boat Club of New York City was America's first Jewish rowing organization (1887). The name synonymous with Jewish rowing on the Olympic level was Allen P. Rosenberg, who coached the 1964 American rowing team to a pair of victories.

Shooting (Yes, I'm serious): One noted star was the publisher of the *Hebrew*, an early Jewish San Francisco newspaper. Philo Jacobi, representing the American Sharpshooters Association of New York, won the Berlin shooting championship in 1868.

Surfing: Yeah, dude, it's true! Jewish South African Shaun Tomson took the 1975 American Championship Cup, followed by the world professional title in 1997.

LET THE "JEWISH" GAMES BEGIN

Jewish athletes come from all over to compete in the Maccabiah Games, often called the Jewish Olympics. The Games, held every four years in Israel, are one of the top sporting events in the world. The movement began in 1895–96 in Constantinople, when the first all-Jewish gymnastics club was started. The first Maccabiah Games were held in 1932 and attracted three hundred athletes from thirteen countries. In 2001, 5,600 competed from over fifty countries. Famous alumni include Mark Spitz, Mitch Gaylord, and Dick Savitt.

Without Them.
WOULD THIS WORLD BE QUITE AS SPORTING?

Harold Abrahams   Sandy Koufax

Barney Ross   Mike Rossman

Fred Lebow   Dick Savitt

Max Baer   Hank Greenberg

ISAAC BERGER   Al Rosen

ARNOLD "RED" AUERBACH

JOE JACOBS   Larry Sherry

Ron Bloomberg   Joey Cornblitt

Howard Cosell   Allie Sherman

Barney Lebrowitz/Battling Levinsky

Lillian Copeland   Bo Belinsky

Benny Friedman   Moe Drabowsky

Abe Saperstein   Ruby Goldstein

Nat Fleischer   Benny Leonard

MARK SPITZ   Ron Mix

Cal Abrams   Hirsch Jacobs

Sid Luckman   MEL ALLEN

JOHN M. BRUNSWICK

Johnny Kling   Maxie Rosenbloom

Lipman Pike   EMANUEL LASKER

Wilhelm Steinitz   Gladys Heldman

Shlomo Glickstein   Irving Jaffee

Senda Berenson   Mitch Gaylord

BARNEY DREYFUSS

CHARLES "BUDDY" MEYER   Eddie Gottlieb

SIDNEY FRANKLIN   Morris Berg

Kenneth Holtzman   Sam Balter

Larry Brown   Nat Holman

Myer Prinstein   ADOLPH "DOLPH" SCHAYES

Dan Daniel   Charlotte Epstein

WILLIAM "RED" HOLTZMAN

Murray Olderman   Bobby Fischer

*All have at least one Jewish parent.

Yiddish and Yinglish

> [Grandmother] used to call me a *shaineh maidel*, which is a "beautiful girl." She died last year. She was ninety years old. And I remember when she died thinking there would be nobody in the world that would ever call me a *shaineh maidel*.
>
> —RABBI JOY LEVITT

MAMA-LOSHEN: A SYMPHONY OF WORDS

Not to be confused with Hebrew, Yiddish, the language of Eastern European Jews, is a hybrid of German, Polish, Russian, Romanian, Ukrainian, and other Slovene dialects. Yiddish became known as *mama-loshen,* "mothers' language," since Jewish women, who were not taught Hebrew, spoke it to their children, who as adults spoke it to Jews from other Eastern European countries in shtetls (little villages)—or on the run. This gave Yiddish its remarkable richness.

> In the Jewish life I knew there was a trinity to whom we appealed or expressed our fears. A small accident would evoke "Mammenyu" (beloved mother), a larger mishap would

bring forth "Tottenyu" (beloved father), and a shock would provoke "Gottenyu" (beloved G-d). A disaster could evoke an appeal to all three. Mother, Father, and G-d represented the core of Jewish family life. Every home depended on the warmth and care given by Mother, the strength and security given by Father, and the omnipresence and omnipotence of G-d. Mother was there when you were ailing or hungry or cold, Father was always handy to protect you, and G-d was available for everything."

—DORE SCHARY,
playwright and producer

VAT ARE YOU TALKING?

First-generation American Jews whose families hailed from Eastern Europe grew up hearing that marvelous "hecscent" whenever *bubbe* (Gram) or *tanta* (Aunt) talked in a colorful mixture of Yiddish and English.

In 1940, Franklin D. Roosevelt was running against Wendell Wilkie.
  "I'm voting for Mendel Vilkie," said Pincus
  "What are you talking? There's no such candidate," said Fein. "It's Wendell Wilkie."
  "In dat case," said Pincus, "I'm voting for Rosenveld."

Note that "Pincus" also turned FDR into a Jewish name, which, whether a slip or an attempt at assimilation, was not uncommon. My own *bubbe* (Gram) swore by Abraham Lin-Cohen and that famous Roman, Sid Caesar. Upon correction, her answer? "Sid . . . Julius . . . ," and shrug. Which meant as long as we knew she knew the difference, why make a fuss? Or Sid and Julius were both smart.

Leonard and Manny were discussing Yiddish when Lenny observed there's no word for "disappointed." Manny couldn't believe it and decided to call his mother.

"Mamaleh," he said in Yiddish, "if I promised to come on Friday, and you worked all day to make me the finest chopped liver, soup, chicken, then, two minutes before I'm supposed to arrive, I call to say something important came up and I can't come, what would you say?"

"Hmmm," She sighed. "I'd say, '*Oy bin ich* (Am I). . . disappointed."

I can recall my own mother asking my *bubbe* how to say "Happy Birthday" in Yiddish. After mulling, she blurted: "Heppy Boyzday!"

Yiddish! It is doubtful there is another language that is quite so brave, anxious, hilarious, bawdy, irreverent, expressive, filled with majesty—and, most of all, sentiment. Which is why it's "catching." So many Yiddish words are now in common usage, we call them Yinglish.

THE STORY OF *Oy*

Never has there been one word that constitutes a whole vocabulary more than the Yiddish *oy*. It can register surprise, pain, relief, despair, or horror. The meaning varies from "*Oy*, I gained five pounds" to "The IRS is auditing? *Oy vay!*" (The *vay* adding more woe to the *oy*.) When in despair it is much more than "too bad." It comes from the *kishkes* (guts), from thousands of years of Jewish trials. A first cousin is *nu*, connoting a frown, a sigh, a grin, a sneer. *Oy* and *nu* together work like a dictionary!

> "*Oy*," says Goldstein.
> "*Oy vay*," says Stern.
> "*Nu?*" says Rosenblatt.
> At which point Horowitz puts on his coat.
> "Listen . . . if you're talking politics, I'm leaving."

• • • • • •

Moskowitz invests in a play, providing he says a line. The director offers: "The king is dead." In rehearsal, Moskowitz delivers in a boring monotone.

"Moskowitz, the king's death is a catastrophe! You're very upset. Got it?" says the director.

"Got it," says Moskowitz.

Again, "The king is dead"—in the same boring monotone.

"Do you have a brother?" says the director.

"Yes. Mendel."

"You love him?"

"Of course!"

"Ah! Now, when you say 'The king is dead,' I want you to think, 'Mendel is dead.' Got it?"

"Got it," says Moskowitz. Once again, "The king is dead," in the same boring monotone—then suddenly Moskowitz, clapping his hands to his cheeks, shrieks, "Oy vay!"

A HIERARCHY OF PITY

Just as there are many words for snow in Alaska, Yiddish has words for every nuance of personality, especially fools and losers. A classic distinction:

The *shlimazel* can be brilliant, an Einstein, but just as he's saying E=MC, lightning will come down, destroy his papers, and render him senseless before he can eek out the "square."

The *shlemiel* can be either a simpleton or unaware—like the professor of Viking literature who can't tie his shoelace, then falls on the *shlimazel*.

Beneath both is the *nebech*—a nonentity. A mister cellophane.

Leo Rosten explained it best: "The *shlemiel* trips, and knocks down the *shlimazel*; and the *nebech* repairs the *shlimazel*'s glasses."

YINGLISH: A QUIZ

As a college student, I was the only Jew in my dorm. By summer the others went home to places like Picawa, Wisconsin, saying, "Oy vay! I can't believe the shlepping I did!" But given the richness, the vastness, the *chutzpah* (guts) of Yiddish, it's not surprising they "caught" it.

How well do you *farshtaist* (understand) Yinglish? Match up!

1. Kvetch	A. Drag/pull; one who looks like he's being dragged, a jerk
2. Nosh	B. Shoddy/ cheap goods
3. Shlep	C. To talk, chatter; also, to butter up
4. Bubee	D. Whine or one who whines or complains
5. Shmooze	E. Money
6. Plotz	F. From "grandmother," now "sweetie"—on shows like Letterman a lot
7. Shlock	G. Burst from joy, hilarity—or aggravation

8. Gelt	H. Snack, to eat a little something
9. Shtick	I. Junk, garbage—in things or food
10. Kibbitz	J. Nothing, beans
11. Bupkes	K. Crazy
12. Shmear	L. Spread, as in cream cheese, or a palm (not nice)
13. Chozzerai	M. To joke, tease, also to meddle
14. Meshugge	N. Cheap piece of clothing; a rag
15. Shmatte	O. A small bit or, in show business, a routine
16. Mensch	P. A human being, but more, a good, decent, noble human being!

1—D; 2—H; 3—A; 4—F; 5—C; 6—G;
7—B; 8—E; 9—O; 10—M; 11—J; 12—L;
13—I; 14—K; 15—N; 16—P

SPEAKING OF CHUTZPAH!

This Yinglishism is beloved by all for its gall, guts, and in-your-face affrontery!

A woman gets on a hot, crowded bus and stands in front of a girl.

Hands across her chest, she sighs. "If you knew what I have, you'd give me your seat." The girl gives her the seat, then takes out a fan.

The woman says, "If you knew what I have, you'd give me that fan." The girl gives her the fan.

Ten minutes later, the woman yells at the driver, "Stop! Let me off!" He says he'll drop her at the next corner.

Hand across her chest, she says, "If you knew what I have, you'd let me out here!" He quickly swerves and opens the door. As she steps out, he asks, "Madam, what is it you have?"

"Chutzpah!" she replies.

• • ● • •

How do you make legalese a little less meshugge? Add a little chutzpah! (So what else is new?) According to Judge Alex Kozinksi and Eugene Volokh the word *chutzpah* has appeared in 112 reported judicial cases, almost all since 1980, suggesting, "there has been a dramatic increase in the actual amount of chutzpah in the U.S." or "Yiddish is quickly supplanting Latin" in legal argot. The first reported judicial application of *chutzpah* was in 1972. Perhaps finding "gall" and "temerity" not quite on the money, the Georgia Court of Appeals used it in a case involving a break-in at a sheriff's office to steal guns. Now that's chutzpah!

—From "Lawsuit, Shmawsuit,"
in the *103 Yale Law Journal* 463
(1993)

My father never lived to see his dream come true of an all-Yiddish-speaking Canada.
—DAVID STEINBERG

Jewish Proverbs

L ie down with dogs, get up with fleas," sighed Bubbe (Grandma) Bella every time the author brought home a date. Oy. And for a wish? "From your mouth to G-d's ears," as per custom, we "poo-ed" our assent. Such is the power of Jewish proverbs. Woven over centuries, they are a tapestry of our warmth, humor, wisdom, and hopes. Based upon common sense and a simple (okay, not so simple) logic, they are loaded with panache and humanity. For, *Tsevishen yidden vert men nit farfalen*: "One does not perish among Jews."

Guests, like fish, begin to stink on the third day.

A boil is fine as long as it's under someone else's arm.

One father can support ten children; but it is difficult for ten children to support one father.

The masses are asses.

A man should stay alive if only out of curiosity.

One lie is a lie, two are lies, but three is politics!

The first time it's smart, the second time it's cute, the third time you get a sock in the teeth.

You can't make cheesecakes out of snow.

Be sure to stay healthy—you can kill yourself later.

I can't sing but I'm an expert on it.

If you're at odds with your Rabbi, make peace with your bartender.

If all men pulled in one direction, the world would topple over.

Better to die upright than to live on your knees.

Without Them,
WOULD THIS WORLD BE
QUITE AS LITERATE?

Leon Uris   Isaac Asimov

Sholem Aleichem   Gertrude Stein

HOWARD FAST   Boris Pasternak

Norman Mailer   Rachel

Leo Rosten   CHAIM POTOK

Dorothy Parker   *ISAAC BASHEVIS SINGER*

ISRAEL JOSHUA SINGER

Budd Schulberg   Calvin Trillin

E. L. Doctorow

Wendy Wasserstein   Herman Wouk

Irwin Shaw   *Simon & Schuster*

J. D. Salinger   Bernard Malamud

Gail Parent   Irving Stone

Jerzy Kosinski   EDNA FERBER

Bennett Cerf   Jules Feiffer   Saul Bellow

Nelly Sachs   JUDY BLUME

IRVING WALLACE   Henry Roth

PHILIP ROTH

NATHANAEL WEST   Nora Ephron

Studs Terkel   Norman Cousins

Joseph Heller   Fran Lebowitz   Mendele

Rod Serling   Robert Sheckley

KARL JAY SHAPIRO   Allen Ginsberg

SUSAN SONTAG   S. J. Perelman

Meyer Levin   Emma Lazarus

Dan Greenburg

Harlan Ellison   Herbert Gold

Harry Golden   Dr. Seuss

Max Shulman   Shel Silverstein

FRANZ KAFKA   S. Y. Agnon

Marcel Proust   Alfred Knopf

Irving Howe   FANNIE HURST

Sholem Asch   Ira Levin

Nadine Gordimer   Sol Yurick   Isaac Babel

MAURICE SENDAK   Lois Gould

Grace Paley   Judith Rossner

*All have at least one Jewish parent.

187

Jewish Curses!

My father—he sort of collected Yiddish curses.
. . . He heard one woman yell at a butcher she
was mad at, "May you have an injury that is
not covered by workmen's compensation."
That was his favorite curse.

—CALVIN TRILLIN

Yiddish is delicious—in humor and hatred.
Listen. "*Er zol vaksen vi a tsibeleh, mit dem kop
in drerd*." No one would translate until I was
twenty-one, then solemnly, "It means . . . 'He
should grow like an onion, with his head in the
ground.'"

Whew. What power Yiddish gave our parents!
An inalienable right to levy unintelligible maledic-
tions upon the next generation! But "a curse is not
a telegram: it doesn't arrive so fast" (proverb). Like
caviar, it must be savored.

**May your blood turn to whiskey so that a
hundred bedbugs get drunk on it and
dance the mazurka in your belly button.**

**May all your teeth fall out except one—and
that should ache you.**

May you fall into the outhouse just as a regiment of Ukrainians is finishing a prune stew and twelve barrels of beer.

May your teeth get angry and chew off your head.

May you have a lot of money but may you be the only one in the family with it.

May you grow two more hands to scratch all your itches.

May you win a lottery, and spend it all on doctors.

May you grow so rich your widow's second husband never has to worry about making a living.

May you back into a pitchfork and grab a hot stove for support.

Onions should grow from your navel.

May you have a mansion with a thousand rooms, and in each room a bed, and you will have such a fever you will roll from bed to bed.

• • • ● • • •

The *Aleph-Baiz* (ABC's) of Jewish Humor

Just as Morey Amsterdam had a joke on every topic, so now do we present you with a Jewish joke for every letter, just in case someone shouts at you, "Quick! A joke! The letter *Q!*"

A: The Affair

Patricia never looked so good. She is permeated with a renewed bloom; her eyes sparkle, her step is light. Her Jewish friend, Ruthie, is amazed.

"How is it, Patricia, you seem to be in such good shape lately?"

Patricia looks around and whispers, "Frankly, Ruthie, . . . I had an affair."

"Really?"

"But listen, Ruthie, . . . it's a secret."

"So, how come you're telling me now?"

"Because, you're my best friend."

"Yeah." Ruthie sniffs. "So how come I wasn't invited?"

B: THE *BUBBE* (GRANDMOTHER)

Bubbe is giving directions by phone to her grandson, who is coming to visit her for the first time in her new condo in Florida with his wife.

"Listen, darling, there's a panel at the front door of the complex. With your elbow push button 14T. I'll buzz you in. Come inside, the elevator is on the right. Get in, and with your elbow hit 14. When you get out I'm on the left. With your elbow, hit my doorbell."

"No problem, Bubbe. . . But why am I hitting all these buttons with my elbow?"

"What? You're coming empty-handed?"

C: THE CREMATION

Mrs. Finkle is preparing her will and calls in her Rabbi.

"I have two requests before I die," she says. "First, I want to be cremated."

"But that's forbidden by Jewish law," the Rabbi says.

"I'm sorry, but I want to be cremated."

After hours of talking and getting nowhere, the Rabbi sighs. "So, what is your second request?"

"I want my ashes scattered in Bloomingdale's."

"Bloomingdale's!" exclaims the Rabbi. "Why Bloomingdale's?"

"That way, I'm sure my daughters will visit me at least twice a week."

D: THE DREAM

Saddam Hussein calls the president early one morning. "I had a wonderful dream last night. I could see America—the whole country—and on each house there was a banner."

"What did it say?" asks the president

"LONG LIVE SADDAM HUSSEIN!"

"You know," says the president, "I'm glad you called, because last night I had a similar dream. I could see all of Baghdad. It was completely rebuilt and beautiful, and on each house there flew an enormous banner too."

"And what did it say?" asks Saddam.

"I don't know," replies the president. "I can't read Hebrew."

E: EGGS

When the millionaire Brodsky came to a small Ukrainian town, all the inhabitants poured out onto the streets to welcome him. With official pomp he was led to the inn, where he ordered two eggs for breakfast. When he finished, the innkeeper asked him for twenty rubles. Brodsky was astonished.

"Are eggs so rare in these parts?" he asked, incredulously.

"No," said the innkeeper quickly. "Brodskys are!"

F: THE FATHER-IN-LAW

Schwartz goes to meet his son-in-law-to-be, Sol, who is very religious.

"*So nu*, tell me, Sol, what do you do?" asks the father-in-law.

"I study Torah," the young man replies.

"Admirable. But how are you going to house and feed my daughter?"

"It will not be a problem. I study Torah, and it says G-d will provide."

"But you'll have children. How will you clothe them?"

"It will not be a problem. G-d will provide."

Schwartz returns home to his wife, who anxiously asks if they got along.

"Of course," says Schwartz. "I only just met him, and already he thinks I'm G-d."

G: The Grave Site

It's the anniversary of Herman Mendelbaum's
death, and his widow decides to go to the
cemetery. But since it's been a while, she's confused and can't find poor Herman's grave. So
the groundskeeper takes her to the office,
where the records are kept. Poring over the
maps and lists, he shrugs. "I'm sorry, but
there's no record of a Herman Mendelbaum
buried here. The closest I can find is a Sadie
Mendelbaum," he says.

"That's him!" she exclaims. "He always put
everything in my name."

H: Hadassah Ladies

A tour bus with thirty Hadassah ladies turned
over, and all were dispatched to heaven.
However, the admitting angel couldn't let them
in because the computers were down.
G-d intervened and asked Satan to provide tem-
porary housing. Soon after, G-d received
an urgent telephone call from Satan telling Him
to take the women off his hands.

"What's the problem?"

Satan replied, "Those Hadassah ladies are
ruining my whole setup. Only two hours
and already they raised $100,000 for an air-
conditioning system!"

I: IRS

Rabbi Schwartz answers his phone.

"Hello, is this Rabbi Schwartz?"

"It is."

"This is the IRS. Can you help us?"

"I can."

"Do you know Sol Rabinowitz?"

"I do."

"Is he a member of your congregation?"

"He is."

"Did he donate ten thousand dollars?"

"He will."

J: Japanese Businessmen

Two Japanese businessmen are talking during their dip in the hot baths at the geisha house.

"Hirokosan, I have unpleasant news for you. Your wife is dishonoring you."

Upset, Hirokosan asks for more information.

"More, she is dishonoring you with a foreigner who is of the Jewish faith."

Shocked, Hirokosan goes home to confront his wife. "I am told you are dishonoring me with a foreigner of the Jewish faith."

"That is a lie!" she replies, outraged. "Where did you hear such *mishegoss* (craziness)?!"

K: KINE-AHORA
(MUMBO JUMBO TO WARD OFF BAD LUCK)

An old Jewish man is on the witness stand.

"How old are you?" asks the D.A.

"I am, *kine-ahora*, eighty-one."

"Please just answer the question!" says the D.A. "Now, how old are you?"

"*Kine-ahora*, eighty-one," the old man repeats.

The judge interrupts. "The witness will answer only the question or be held in contempt!"

At which point the defense lawyer, Goldstein, jumps up. "Your Honor, allow me to ask the question." He turns to the old man, "*Kine-ahora*, how old are you?"

"Eighty-one!" says the old man.

L: LONDON

Horowitz stops at a posh gourmet shop in London. A salesman in morning coat approaches.

"Can I help you, sir?"

"I would like a pound of lox."

"Sir," replies the salesperson stiffly, "I believe you mean smoked salmon."

"Whatever. Also blintzes."

"I believe you mean crepes, sir."

"Sure. Okay. Make it a dozen," says Horowitz. "And a pound of chopped liver."

"I think," says the salesperson, sighing, "you mean pâté."

"All right already, pâté. And," adds Horowitz, "I'd like you to deliver to my house today."

"Sorry, sir," retorted the indignant salesperson. "But we don't *shlep* on Shabbes!"

M: MAYBE ONE IN A MILLION

Goldberg walked to the top of a hill to talk to G-d:

"G-d, what's a million years to you?"

And G-d said, "A minute."

Then Goldberg asked, "Well, what's a million dollars to you?"

And G-d said, "A penny."

Then Goldberg asked, "G-d, may I have a penny?"

And G-d said, "Sure. In a minute."

N: THE NEGOTIATION

Solly and Max are describing their fishing expeditions to each other with great relish.

"Once in Florida, " says Solly, "I caught a fish so huge it took three men to shlep it in!"

"That's nothing," scoffs Max. "In New England, I once caught a lamp with a date engraved on it—1492—the year Christopher Colombus discovered America!"

"Big deal," says Solly rising from his chair. "My fish weighed 150 pounds."

"Yeah? The lamp I caught was still lit!"

Nose to nose, the two stare each other down. Until finally . . .

"Listen, Max," says Solly. "How about . . . my fish weighs only five pounds, and you put your light out!"

O: THE OPTIMIST

A group of retired men gather each morning at a café, drink their tea, and discuss the world siuation. Given the state of the world, their talks are usually depressing.

One day, out of the blue, one of the men announces, "You know what? I am an optimist."

The others are shocked, but then one of them notices something fishy. "Wait a minute! If you're such an optimist why do you always look so worried?"

"What? You think it's easy being an optimist?"

P: THE POISON

A very upset Seymour goes to see the Rabbi. "Something terrible is happening!"

"What's the matter!" asks the Rabbi.

"I think my wife is poisoning me!"

"Now, Seymour, how can that be?"

"I'm telling you, Bernice is poisoning me!"

"All right, all right. Tell you what, let me talk with her. I'll see what I can find out and let you know," says the skeptical Rabbi.

A week later the Rabbi calls Seymour. "Well, I spoke to your wife. I called Bernice on the phone, and she talked for four hours. You want my advice?"

"Of course!" says Seymour.

"Take the poison."

Q: A QUIZ

If 5762 is the year according to the Jewish calendar,

and 4700 is the year according to the Chinese calendar,

what is 1062?

Answer: The total number of years that Jews went without Chinese food.

R: RSVP

Old Man Finkelstein and his wife were stuck.
They just received an invitation to a very hoo-
ha wedding but couldn't figure out the meaning of the abbreviation RSVP.

"Oy, Meyer, if only our son, the college
graduate, was here, he'd know." Mrs.
Finkelstein sighed as she kissed her husband
good-bye.

"RSVP, RSVP . . ." She pondered it all day
and suddenly raced to call Meyer at work.

"I figured it out!" she said, beaming.
" 'RSVP' means 'Remember Send Vedding
Present!' "

S: SOLOMON-IN-LAW

A Jewish town had a shortage of grooms, so
they had to import them. One day a
groom-to-be arrived by train, and two prospec-
tive mothers-in-law, Bella and Dora, were waiting, each claiming ownership of him for her
daughter. The Rabbi was called to solve the
problem.

"There is only one solution," said the Rabbi.
"We shall divide him in two and give each of
you a piece."

At this, Bella threw up her hands, screaming,
"No! Give him to Dora!"

"Ah ha!" said the Rabbi. "Done! The one willing to cut him in half is the *real* mother-in-law!"

T: *TRAIF* (FORBIDDEN FOOD)

A Rabbi is dying to taste pork after hearing for years talk of chops, never mind spare ribs. So he flies to a remote island and orders the most expensive pork dish on the menu.

As he eagerly waits, he hears his name called. Who does he see but ten members of his Congregation, who, his luck, are dining in this same spot. Just then the waiter appears with a tray carrying a huge roasted pig with an apple in its mouth.

As his congregants stare, the Rabbi, thinking fast, says, "Oy! Order an apple in this place and look how they serve it?"

U: UN

At a UN Mideast meeting, the Israeli ambassador says: "Before my speech, an old story. . . . When Moses led the Jews out of Egypt, he went through deserts and the people grew thirsty. So Moses waved his cane and a pond appeared. Moses wished to cleanse his body, so he dove into the waters. When he emerged, his clothing was stolen. And I believe the Palestinians stole those clothes—"

At which point, Yasir Arafat screams, "This is a travesty! There were no Palestinians there at that time!"

"And with that in mind," says the Israeli, "I shall now begin my speech."

V: THE VERANDA

Goldberg, now rich, is showing his country estate to his old friend Bloom from the Bronx.

Goldberg sighs. "After a lifetime in the city, what a pleasure to be here with the fresh air. But the best thing? Lying on my veranda. Such a delight, my veranda! Oy, how I love my beautiful veranda!"

Back in the Bronx, Bloom, shaking his head, reports to his wife. "I think something happened to Goldberg's wife."

"With Rachael? What?" asks his wife.

"I never saw her. I think maybe Goldberg got rid of her and now has a Gentile woman—named Veranda."

W: THE WIFE

Ginsberg, mayor of an Israeli town, passes a construction site with his wife. A construction worker calls out to the woman. "Sara . . . how are you!"

"Avi! Nice to see you again," she replies. Then she introduces her husband. After a short chat, they continue on.

"How do you know such a man?" asks the mayor.

"We were sweethearts in school. I almost married him."

He laughs. "See how lucky you are? If I hadn't married you, today you would be married to a construction worker!"

"If I had married him," says his wife, "so now *he'd* be the mayor."

X: WHAT'S IN A NAME?

Stein, who knew no English, opened a bank account and signed with two X's. A year later, having done very well for himself, he came once again to the bank with a big deposit.

"Mr. Stein," said the teller, "why do you now use three X's?"

"Not me . . . my wife," he said. "Now that we're rich, she wants me to take a middle name."

Y: YESHIVA UNIVERSITY

Yeshiva University formed a crew team. Though they practiced for hours and hours, they always came in dead last. Finally they sent Yankel to spy on the Harvard team. He shlepped to Cambridge and hid by the Charles River to watch them practice. After two days, he returned.

"I finally figured out how they do it," said Yankel, excited, to his eager teammates. "They have *eight* fellows rowing and only *one* fellow screaming!"

Z: THE *ZAYDE* (GRANDPA)

Milton's wife nagged him to go to a seance at Madame Frieda's so he could talk to his beloved *zayde*. At the next seance they sat holding hands around a table.

Suddenly Madame Frieda's eyes bobbed open. "Is that . . . Milton's *zayde* I hear?"

"Zayde!" cried Milton.

"Milteleh," a voice quavered.

"Yes! This is your Milty! Zayde, are you happy?"

"Bliss! With your *bubbe* (grandma) together, we laugh, we sing . . ."

A dozen questions Milty asked until, "Milteleh, an angel calls. Only one more question."

"Zayde," asked Milty, "when did you learn to speak English?"

Enter Right: Theater

Next to life, next to education (all right, next to food), the Jews have had a long love affair with the theater, in Yiddish and in English.

· · · ● · ·

Although early pious Jews refrained from all stage activity, by the first century some Jews could be found performing on the pagan stage. In Rome, among Nero's favorites was the Jewish actor Aliturus, and the first "stand-up" may have been a man named Menophilus. In the third century, Resh Lakish, a Jewish scholar, paid the bills by performing as a circus strongman.

Okay, So Neil Simon He Wasn't—But . . .

One of the earliest minor American-born playwrights was also one of the most influential Jews in the country in the beginning of the nineteenth century. Mordecai Manuel Noah, the son of a wealthy patriot, was a lawyer, a judge, a journalist, a military man, and an ardent utopian who envisioned a Jewish colony (Ararat) on an island in the Niagara River near Buffalo—almost a hundred years before Theodor Herzl. A prolific, if not terrific playwright, he wrote plays like *She Would Be a Soldier* (1819) reflecting his patriotic zeal. However, unlike some of his other ventures, his scribbles met with bad luck and generally not-so-great reviews. The night his *Siege of Tripoli* was supposed to premiere, the theater burned down (Noah donated the box office to the actors), and in the *Grecian Captive,* the actors almost brought themselves—and the house—down when the elephant upon which they were entering got a little spooked.

THE YIDDISH THEATER

For the immigrant, the Yiddish theater was part theater, part social center. You went to laugh, to cry, and to *shmooze* (chat).

> The stars of the Yiddish theater were my heroes. David Kessel, Ludwig Zatz, Menashe Skulnik, Boris Tomashefsky, Molly Picon, Jacob Kalish, and Muni Weisenfreund, who went on to become Paul Muni. Yiddish theaters were all over New York City. Around 1935, on a given Friday night, people would have a choice of twenty-six theaters to go to. Live shows, a drama, a musical. . . . Women who worked as seamstresses for nine, ten dollars a week, would put on the one good dress they owned. . . . and go . . . to have a good cry. It was a tremendous event.
>
> —AL LEWIS, actor

The first two Yiddish amateur plays we know of were *Reb Hennoch; or, What to Do About It* by Yitskhok Euchel (1793) and *Frivolity and Religiosity* by Aaron Wolfsohn (1796). Written in Germany, they ridicule superstition in the shtetl (small village). However, the father of the Yiddish theater was Avrom Goldfadn. Starting in 1876, he wrote and produced the first professional plays in Eastern Europe. Under his guidance and troupes the Yiddish theater gained definition.

Between 1881 and 1903 over a million Yiddish-speaking immigrants arrived in America, mostly settling on the Lower East Side of New York. Yiddish theater followed in 1882, thanks to talents like Boris Thomashefsky and the Golubok Brothers. Among many spawns were Jacob P. Adler (who spawned Celia, Luther, and Stella), Sigmund Mogulesko, David Kessler, Bertha Kalich—and huge rivalries among companies. If Kessler wore a hat, Adler wore a bigger one with a feather. If one killed an enemy, another killed an army. The Yiddish theater contributed great culture and stars like Paul Muni, Molly Picon, and Menashe Skulnik. In recognition, Mayor Abe Beame proclaimed December 5, 1976, Yiddish Theater Day in New York City.

· · · ● · ·

The great Yiddish theater actress Molly Picon was once starring on Second Avenue and packing in the crowds. Two women approached the box office and were told they were sold out.

"But we came all the way from Long Island," complained one lady, lamenting the trip into New York City.

"I'm sorry," said the man at the box office, "but there's not a single seat left."

"It's things like this," said the other woman, "that's killing the Jewish theater!"

· · · ● · ·

One day before the Stratford Shakespeare Festival, Isadore Hershberg showed up to audition, telling the director, "I vant to be en hectah. I vant to play Hemlet."

"You want to be an actor?" asked the startled director. "I'm sorry . . . perhaps a walk-on part—"

"No!" interrupted the old man. "Hemlet, dot's vat I vant!"

"Okay," said the director, chuckling, as the old man stepped onto the stage.

All was quiet.

Then in deep, resonant tones, speaking in perfect English diction, Isadore Hershberg recited the immortal "To be or not to be, that is the question. Whether 'tis nobler . . . "

The director, cast, and crew stood spellbound. When the old man finished, the director exclaimed, "Why . . . that is fantastic!"

"No, boychick," Isadore replied, "dot's hecting!"

· · · ● · · ·

I KNOW YOU! YOU'RE WHAT'S HIS NAME!

Arthur Miller, the famous playwright, was standing in a bar when a man entered, nattily dressed, and stared.

"Miller, Arthur Miller! . . . Solly Fishbein from the old high school."

With great effort, Miller remembered. "Yes," he mumbled, "of course—"

"How many years has it been?" said Solly. "And here I am, married, two kids, in the clothing business, and making a damned good thing out of it, too. . . . Living it up. . . . And my kids. . . . The older one is at MIT . . ."

Finally, Solly asked, "What have you been doing?"

"I write," said Miller.

"Advertising?"

"I write plays," said Miller.

"Ever . . . been produced?"

"Well," said Miller. "I suppose the play I wrote that's best known is *Death of a Salesman*."

"*Death of a* . . ." After a pause, Solly said in a subdued voice, "Pardon me, Arthur Miller, but are you—*Arthur Miller*?"

· · ● · ·

CURTAIN CALLS

Jewish playwrights have been responsible for creating some of the theater's most enduring works.

Classics all, can you match the play with the author?

Plays	Playwrights
1. *The Little Foxes*	A. David Mamet
2. *Awake and Sing*	B. Arthur Miller
3. *Dinner at Eight*	C. George S. Kaufman and Edna Ferber
4. *The Crucible*	D. Paddy Chayefsky
5. *The Front Page*	E. Lillian Hellman
6. *The Caretaker*	F. Moss Hart and George S. Kaufman
7. *American Buffalo*	G. Ben Hecht
8. *Marty*	H. Tony Kushner
9. *The Man Who Came to Dinner*	I. Harold Pinter
10. *Angels in America*	J. Clifford Odets

1-E; 2-J; 3-C; 4-B; 5-G; 6-I; 7-A; 8-D; 9-F; 10-H

Without Them,
WOULD THIS WORLD INSPIRE
US WITH AS MUCH VISION?

Steven Spielberg   Avrom Goldfadn   Neil Simon

Louis B. Mayer   IRVING THALBERG

ABE BURROWS   Adolph Zukor

DAVID SARNOFF   David O. Selznick

LEWIS SELZNICK   William Fox

ELIZABETH SWADOS   MARCUS LOEW

Barry Levinson   The Shuberts

George Cukor   Otto Preminger

David Merrick   Billy Wilder   Samuel Goldwyn

Moss Hart   George S. Kaufman

Edna Ferber   Stanley Kubrick

Norman Lear   WILLIAM PALEY

Sir Lew Grade   Harold Pinter   Harry Cohn

Mike Nichols   ROB REINER

WARNER BROTHERS   David Mamet

ARTHUR MILLER   Sherry Lansing

HARRY HOUDINI   Shari Lewis

Lorne Michaels   Mel Tolkin

Ben Hecht   Emanuel Azenberg   Hal Prince

Mark Goodson   **IRNA PHILLIPS**

CLIFFORD ODETS   **Lillian Hellman**

LARRY GELBART   Mike Todd   Jesse Lasky

Billy Rose   David Susskind   *Dore Schary*

Florenz Ziegfeld   Howard Koch

Joseph & Herman Mankiewicz

ERICH VON STROHEIM   **Tony Kushner**

Dennis Prager   *Sol Yurok*

Michael Thomshefsky   ARTHUR LAURENTS

David Belasco   **Alexander Cohen**

Sol Hurok   **Bruce Jay Friedman**

Carl Laemmle   **WILLIAM FRIEDKIN**

Harvey & Bob Weinstein   Lewis Milestone

Sydney Pollack   *JOSEPH STEIN*

Dawn Steel   **Paddy Chayefsky**

Herb Gardner   Israel Horovitz   JOSEPH SCHILDKRAUT

Robert Wise   William Wyler

Fred Zinnemann   Franklin Schaffner

---

*All have at least one Jewish parent.

Essen! Essen! (Eat! Eat!)

What a Jew loves more even than a great joke is a great meal.

> Jews are the only people who eat while they're getting ready to eat. They eat at a smorgasbord like horses, but they don't count that as food because they didn't sit down. "I was walking around, so I took some. And besides I ate it from a cardboard plate—it wasn't a real plate, I didn't take a real fork. The fact that it wound up in my mouth . . . I didn't expect it, it happened." It's not even called eating. It just winds up in your mouth while you're walking.
>
> —JACKIE MASON

Most of our kosher "deli" started as dishes of the poor in Eastern Europe. Some even got "classy."

> Chicken any which-way, gefilte fish, chopped liver—*we* created all that. Don't let the French tell you about pâté! They got the pâté from us! *We* made the pâté. They got their pâté but we had our pâté. And our pâté was even better

than their pâté! . . . . My grandmother—may she rest in peace—never knew . . . about recipes. They did it all by heart, they never measured. They did it all with their fingertips and it was delicious—delicious! I still can't get the boiled beef like she used to make. There's an art to that. *We* created boiled beef. . . . There was a lot of fat involved. So from that we used to get the gout. *We* created the gout. That's *our* disease.

—FYVUSH FINKEL

• • • ● • • •

Not only are Jewish foods mouth-watering, heartburn-producing delights but from their names alone you can chuckle. Face it. *White bread* just doesn't deliver the same punch as, say, *knish* or *farfel*. How much do you know about them? Take the following quiz.

ULTIMATE (OKAY, WHATEVER) JEWISH FOOD TEST

Match these foods to something they (probably) contain.

1. Blintzes	A.	Barley-size noodlets—put a twinkle in your soup
2. Challah	B.	Thin rolled pancake filled with cheese, fruit, or meat—a Jewish crepe
3. Cholent	C.	Rendered fat—heartburn: the liquid version
4. Farfel	D.	Sabbath oven dish cooked overnight, includes beans or meat—feeds an army
5. Gribenes	E.	Cracklings from rendered fats—Jewish popcorn while waiting for the angioplasty
6. Shmaltz	F.	Sabbath twists of bread, like cake—slice only if Reformed
7. Kugel	G.	Unleavened bread, perforated. When wet, could be used for mortar

8. Matzah
H. Jewish haggis—literally "intestines," now beef casings stuffed with veggies and spices

9. Kasha varnishkes
I. Noodle or potato pudding—on day two like the scales of a prehistoric animal

10. Kishka
J. Round or square noodle dough, filled with cheese or meat, for soup—to Sam Levinson, "meatballs with sport jackets"

11. Kreplach
K. Buckwheat groats with bow-tie noodles—the *varnish* is only in the saying

12. Bagel
L. Soup "nuts"—egg-and-flour Ping-Pong balls

13. Latke
M. Pudding/stew of veggies, often carrots—also everything else

14. Knishes
N. To Leo Rosten, doughnuts with a college education—Yeshiva University

15. Mondlen	O.	Smoked salmon—comes not salty or like the Dead Sea
16 Tsimmes	P.	Potato or kasha dumplings—no boardwalk should be without it
17. Lox	Q.	Stuffed fish, like U-boats—sweet or sour
18. Gefilte fish	R.	Potato pancake—fried in enough oil to power a Hummer

1—B; 2—F; 3—D; 4—A; 5—E; 6—C;
7—I; 8—G; 9—K; 10—H; 11—J; 12—N;
13—R; 14—P; 15—L; 16—M; 17—O;
18—Q

Over fifteen correct and you're a *mavin* (expert)! As a reward, take yourself over to . . .

Jews always know two things: suffering and where to find good Chinese food.

—MY FAVORITE YEAR (1982)

Quiz: Where did JFK Jr. go to fill up with pals after he passed his bar exam?

To what was John Glenn referring when he said, "I had more room in the space capsule!"

Where did Roseanne sing—and was appreciated?

If you said a table at Sammy's Roumanian Steak House, give yourself an egg cream!

At this institution on the Lower East Side, you get Yiddish, nostalgic music, an open mike, a table with shmaltz, roasted peppers, sour tomatoes, and all manner of pickles. Owner Stan Zimmerman, who likens it to "a visit to *bubbe's* (grandma's), with relatives of all nationalities who have one thing in common—they're smiling," tells us his favorite things to serve at Sammy's:

1. Chopped liver (Jewish pâté) made with chicken livers and shmaltz mixed like a Caesar salad

2. Potato latkes

3. Roumanian tenderloin, because it's from the four-quarter (Kosher part) and so flavorful

4. Mashed potatoes with gribenes, shmaltz, and pepper

5. The check

Some celebrity favorites at Sammy's:

Dick Clark, Billy Crystal, and Chuck Barris are "Roumanian tenderloin" men. Billy also loves the lamb chops.

Roseanne goes for rib steak.

THE MAKING OF THE EGG CREAM!

Also on Sammy's table are the ingredients to make your own egg cream, an art much debated. Stan Zimmerman settles it once and for all!

Ingredients: Seltzer (from bottle only, green or clear), Fox's U-Bet chocolate syrup (1954 was a good year), whole milk.

1. Put milk in first! (An inch.)

2. Shpritz seltzer almost to the top.

3. Let sit 3 seconds . . . add a little more seltzer.

4. Pour syrup down center of glass, to taste (about ¾ ounce).

5. Stir right, then left.

6. It's done after homogenizing, then separating into a clear, snow white head.

Sorry . . . the author left for a nosh. . . .

Yiddishe Mamas
(Jewish Mothers)

Whether Jewish, Italian, Irish—whatever—who doesn't have one? Okay, maybe the British. However, the author recalls a magazine with a photo of the queen and the word *OY!* during her annus horribilis, when the royal offspring were flying faster than colonies. In Judaism parents place great emphasis on dedicating time to their children. So, our relationships with our mothers?

"Intense."

Tensions are running high in the Weinbaum house. Screaming and fighting are constantly going on between Mrs. Weinbaum and her fourteen-year-old, Jerome, so she brings him to a psychoanalyst.

"So, Doctor, what's his problem?" she asks after two sessions.

"Your son, madam," he tells her, "has an Oedipus complex."

"Oedipus, Shmoedipus," says Mrs. Weinbaum. "As long as he loves his mother."

It was my mother who could accomplish anything, who herself had to admit that it might
even be that she was actually too good. . . .
She could make Jell-O . . . peaches hanging in
it . . . in defiance of the law of gravity. . . .
Weeping, suffering, she grated her own horseradish. . . . She watched the butcher, as she
put it, "like a hawk," to be certain that he did
not forget to put her chopped meat through
the kosher grinder. She would telephone all
the other women in the building drying
clothes on the back lines . . . to tell them
rush, take in the laundry, a drop of rain had
fallen . . . . What radar on that woman! . . .
For mistakes, she checked my sums; for holes,
my socks; for dirt, my nails, my neck, every
seam and crease of my body. . . . She is never
ashamed of her house; a stranger could walk
in and open any closet, any drawer. . . . You
could even eat off her bathroom floor, if that
should ever become necessary.

—PHILIP ROTH
Portnoy's Complaint

• • ● ● • •

A Classic

Mrs. Pushnik sent her son off to his first day of school.

"Now, *bubeleh* (sweetie), be good and listen to the teacher. At lunchtime eat all your food and play nice with the other children, okay, *bubeleh*? Oy, I'm so proud of my *bubeleh*!"

That afternoon, when the little boy returned home, his mother cried: "*Bubeleh*! So, tell me, you learned something at school today?"

"Yeah," said the boy. "I learned my name is Irving."

. . . ● . .

There is a definite connection between being funny and being Jewish. The toughest room I ever played was my mother's kitchen.
—RICHARD BELZER

. . . ● . .

HOW TO BE A JEWISH MOTHER ACCORDING TO DAN GREENBURG: SEX AND MARRIAGE

There are only two things a Jewish Mother needs to know about sex and marriage:

1. Who is having sex?

2. Why aren't they married?

Since . . . everyone in the world is determined to have *some* kind of sex, it will therefore be your duty to make sure that everyone in the world gets married.

The Son

At the age of eight or nine . . . develop in him . . . the good grooming habits which will help him to win the hand of a capable young woman. . . .

"Stand up straight and don't slouch—what girl in her right mind is going to marry a hunchback?" . . .

By age twelve . . . arrange a party for Young People at your home. . . . Smooth the way over those . . . embarrassing moments by introducing him yourself:

"This is my son Marvin who stands like a hunchback."

—DAN GREENBURG,
How to Be a Jewish Mother

DAVID KOLOWITZ WANTS TO BE A SOMETHING
(Ronald Colman, not a pharmacist)

HE GETS HIS CHANCE. AT THE SEEDY MARLOWE THEATER. FOR FIVE DOLLARS. HE PAYS. HE HAS NO IDEA "ENTER LAUGHING!" IS A STAGE DIRECTION. IT IS THE 1930S. PA WONDERS MAYBE THIS ACTING IS ONLY A STAGE—"LIKE MODEL AIRPLANES."

Ma: I think we should . . . send David to pharmacy school right now. . . . Morris, listen . . .—a sickness, the sooner you stop it, the better. . . .

David: . . . I'm going to be an actor. . . . I hate druggists! . . .

Ma: . . . You do whatever you want . . . our feelings don't matter. . . . Papa and me don't matter . . .

David: Okay, okay, I'll be a druggist. . . .

Ma: Whatever you want. . . .

Ah, but David is determined. Continued . . .

DAVID'S OPENING NIGHT

*EXCEPT FOR CRASHING THROUGH A WALL AND
HIS LIPS MOVING WITHOUT A SOUND, DAVID,
ACCORDING TO PA AND MA (WHO FIGURED
OUT, AND CAME) WAS* "THE BEST ONE."

David: . . . I like it, Ma. It's what I like.

Ma: But if it's a mistake?

David: Then it's my mistake. Okay? . . .

Ma: (*Pats him*) David, haven't I always said . . .
whatever you want!

. . .

David (*alone, looks around the stage*): Hello. . . .
My name is David Kolowitz. . . . I'm an
actor.

—JOSEPH STEIN,
Enter Laughing (1963),
adapted from the
semiautobiographical novel
by Carl Reiner

Three Jewish women in Miami are bragging about their devoted sons.

Mrs. Cohen says, "Mine is so devoted he bought me a cruise around the world. First-class."

Mrs. Lapidus counters, "Mine is more devoted. On my birthday, three hundred people he flew in from Brooklyn—and catered!"

Mrs. Fine sniffs. "You want to hear devoted? Three times a week my son, Marvin, goes to a psychiatrist. A hundred and twenty dollars an hour he pays Dr. Shlockman. And what does he talk about the whole time? Me!"

Speaking of Dr. Shlockman . . . *Yiddishe* mamas—and then some.

Finally, after ten years of therapy, Dr. Shlockman feels Marvin is ready to go it alone. A few days go by, and Marvin calls the doctor in a state of hysteria at noon on a Sunday.

"Doctor, I need you! I just took a nap and dreamed you were my mother! Doctor, what does this mean?"

"Now, Marvin," says the shrink, "calm down and we'll figure it out. Tell me, what were you doing just before you took the nap?"

"Well, let's see. I grabbed some breakfast— a Hershey bar and a root beer—"

"A Hershey bar and a root beer? *That* you call breakfast!"

My mother thought everything I did was perfect. And if I was scolded in school, she'd go to the school and scold the teacher. In fact when I was elected to Congress, election night, she said, "I always knew Bella would make it. Because she always did her homework and practiced her violin without being asked to do so." In addition to which [when asked] "How do you account for Bella's success?"

"I was always there," she said. "I was there." And indeed she was.

—BELLA ABZUG,
the first Jewish woman
elected to Congress

Born: August 12, thirty years ago. . . . "So, it's a girl, Manny? You know what that means, you have to pay for the wedding. . . ." One day old! One day old, and they're talking about weddings. . . . A Jewish mother wants her sons out of the Army and her daughters down the aisle.

—GAIL PARENT,
*Sheila Levine Is Dead
and Living in New York*

"How few were her pleasures
She never cared for fashion styles
Her jewels and treasures
She found them in her baby's smiles
Oh I know that I owe what I am today
To that dear little lady so old and grey,
To that wonderful Yiddishe momma,
Momma mine."

This ends (on the highest, most wailing note you could hear with the human ear) perhaps the most heart-wrenching song ever composed about Jewish mothers, "My Yiddishe Momma." It was written in 1925 by Jack Yellen (lyrics) and Ben Pollack (music) and popularized by Sophie Tucker. Although "shmaltzy" by today's standards, it's not hard to understand the wellspring of tears it brought forth from *kinder* (children) and mothers alike, given the hardships that Jewish mothers—often overburdened and uprooted—had to endure not so very long ago.

There's no escaping . . . a few have tried. But, as my own, Jewish mother used to say, "I have radar." And she did.

. . . . ● . .

Mrs. Bloom sets out from her home in Brooklyn for India. After taking the subway to the airport, she boards a plane with two stopovers. Then, from the airport, she gets on a van and asks the driver where to rent a donkey. On the donkey she travels over hilltops, and across valleys, and finally arrives at her destination. She shleps to the top of a steep mountain, to the ashram of the guru, Baba Ganesh.

"I gotta see him," she tells an assistant.

"But that is impossible," he replies. "Nobody may see the Great Guru for the next six months."

"Listen, mistah—I gotta see him," the old woman cries, but the assistant is adamant.

So she sits at the doorstep without food or water for three days.

Desperate, the assistant reluctantly concedes. "You may see our leader, but you must promise to say no more than three words. Will you agree?"

"All right—three words."

And Mrs. Bloom is led down a long marble hall until they come to a far room covered in ancient tapestry. A young man is sitting on a bamboo mat in a yoga position, chanting, "*Om chanti.*"

The woman steps in front of him and says, "*Come home, Sheldon.*"

THE TABLE: 1949

Kate (the mother): My grandfather made this table. With his own hands. For my grandmother. . . . Over fifty-two years she had this table. . . . When I was a little girl, I'd go to her house and she'd let me help her polish it. . . .

When she died, she left a will. . . . But she knew what I wanted. The table you eat on means everything. It's the one time in the day the whole family is together. . . . This is where you share things. . . . People who eat out all the time don't get to be a family.

—NEIL SIMON,
Broadway Bound (1986)

On the *Shadchen*
(Matchmaker) and the
Shidech (the Match!)

A *shadchen* is walking down the beach when a slimy green creature with three eye stalks and huge claws comes crawling out of the surf. The *shadchen* takes off running, then thinks about it and runs back. "Say," she yells at the monster. "Have I got a girl for you!"

A PERFECT MATCHMAKER?

For generations, the *shadchen* (matchmaker) saw the bringing together of worthy couples as a pious calling, and initially the most learned performed this honorable task. As time went on, the image of the *shadchen* suffered, and, as with Dolly Levi in *Hello Dolly*, and Yente, in *Fiddler on the Roof*, the reputation for good-natured but colorful exaggeration prevailed. *(Okay,* think used car salesmen in Tijuana.)

A Classic

A *shadchen*, having sung the praises of a particular female, set up a match with a worthy male. The bridegroom pulls the *shadchen* over.

"You faker, you swindler!" he whispers, furious. "You said she was young; she's fifty if she's a day! You said she was beautiful; she looks like a duck! You said she was shapely, she's built like a plow horse! You said—"

"Listen, you don't have to whisper," interrupts the *shadchen*, "She's also deaf!"

· · · ● · ·

"She looks terrible," the young man reported to the *shadchen*. "How could I marry a woman who looks like that?"

"Look," replied the *shadchen*, "either you like Picasso or you don't!"

JEWISH PERSONAL ADS

Sincere rabbinical student, 27. Enjoys Yom Kippur, Tish'a B'Av, Taanis Esther, Tzom Gedaliah, Asarah B'Teves, Shiva Asar B'Tammuz [mostly days of fasting]. Seeks companion for living life in the "fast" lane.

Nice Jewish guy, 38. No skeletons. No baggage. No personality.

You're probably wondering why an accomplished Ph.D. . . . and Rhodes Scholar like me isn't married yet. I'm a mieskeit [ugly].

Attractive Jewish woman, 35, college graduate, seeks successful Jewish Prince Charming to get me out of my parents' house.

Desperately seeking shmoozing! Retired senior citizen desires female companion 70+ for kvetching [complaining], kvelling [gloating], krechtzing [groaning]. Under 30 is also OK.

Couch potato latke [pancake], in search of the right applesauce. Let's try it for eight days. Who knows?

Are you the girl I spoke with during kiddish [blessings over bread and wine] after shul [synagogue] last week? You excused yourself to get more horseradish for your gefilte fish, but you never returned. How can I contact you again? (I was the one with the cholent [baked food] stain on my tie).

Jewish Princess, 28, seeks successful businessman of any major Jewish denomination: hundreds, fifties, twenties.

• • • ● • •

Jewish businessman, 49, manufactures Sabbath
candles, Hannukah candles, havdallah candles,
Yahrzeit candles. Seeks nonsmoker.

Torah scholar, long beard, payos [earlocks].
Seeks same in woman.

Divorced Jewish man, seeks partner to attend
shul [synagogue] with, light Shabbes candles,
celebrate holidays, build Sukkah together,
attend brisses, Bar Mitzvahs. Religion not
important.

I am a sensitive Jewish prince whom you can
open your heart to. Share your innermost
thoughts and deepest secrets. Confide in me.
I'll understand your insecurities. No fatties,
please.

Israeli professor, 41, with 18 years of teaching in my behind. Looking for American-born woman who speaks English very good.

Jewish male, 34, very successful, smart, independent, self-made. Looking for girl whose father will hire me.

WHY IS THIS WEDDING DIFFERENT FROM ALL OTHER WEDDINGS?

Most people, Jew and non-Jew alike, have seen the famous (and sometimes dicey) custom of the groom stepping on and breaking the wineglass at the conclusion of the Jewish wedding. This dramatic, sweet, and, yes, amusing part of the ceremony has many explanations, ranging from scaring away demons to symbolizing the fragility of joy. Less known is the fact that at a traditional Jewish wedding the question "Who gives this woman away?" is not asked. The reason? Because the Jewish bride is seen as the responsible party making her own commitment, rather than being transferred from the custody of her father to her husband. (In the case of the groom and his mother, however—the author, for one, wouldn't open the topic.)

A TITANIC LOVE STORY

Leonardo Di Caprio and Kate Winslet had little on Isador and Ida Straus. Isador, the Bavarian Jew who, with his brother Nathan, purchased R. H. Macy's in 1896, building it into one of the world's largest retail chains, was also an adviser to President Cleveland, served in Congress, helped found an endowment fund for the Jewish Theological Seminary—and was, alas, a passenger on the ill-fated *Titanic,* which sank on April 14, 1912.

Because of his age (sixty-seven), he was allowed to depart with the women and children, but he refused any special treatment. He urged his wife, Ida, to board a lifeboat, but she, too, declined, reportedly saying, "We have been living together for many years, and where you go, I go."

Over forty-thousand attended their memorial service, and their story was told in a Yiddish song by Solomon Smulewitz.

On Synagogues and Symbols

AND WE SHALL PRAY IN THIS NEW WORLD

The first synagogue in America was erected in 1730 in what is now downtown Manhattan by Congregation Shearith Israel. It was rebuilt several times, and the congregation remains active to this day. Touro, the oldest existing synagogue, owes a debt to Roger Williams, the Puritan minister who established the colony of Rhode Island. With its charter separating church and state, it became a haven for religious minorities. The Congregation, Jeshuath Israel, was founded in 1658. Ground for Touro was broken on August 1, 1759, and dedicated in 1763. Aaron Lopez, the Merchant Prince of New England, who loaned his hundred ships to the service of America, laid the cornerstone. Visitors can tour this Newport, Rhode Island, synagogue, which has been declared a national shrine.

• • • ● • •

The largest synagogue in the world is Temple Emanu-El on Sixty-fifth Street and Fifth Avenue in New York City, with an area of 37,928 square feet. When the Temple's three other sanctuaries and adjoining Chapel are used, the synagogue can accommodate 5,500 people. In 1928 the cornerstone for

238

the new Temple was laid. Within it was placed a metal box containing, among other things, Bibles, volumes I and II of the Union Prayer Book, lists of the Congregation's membership, and a silver Torah pointer. At the ceremony, the president of the Temple, Louis Marshall, said, "Here Mercy and Truth must meet together, and Righteousness and Peace must kiss each other. Here Justice and Charity and the love of one's fellow man must be the line and plummet by which right living is to be attained."

WITH TEN YOU GET—AN EXORCISM

Inspired by the classic play *The Dybbuk* (The Demon), Paddy Chayefsky's *The Tenth Man* deals with mysticism, love, and community. As in *Marty* and *Network*, Chayefsky's ear for language and the "ordinary" lifts the playwright to the "remarkable." In this excerpt, a poor congregation in Mineola, Long Island, is trying to gather a quorum of ten Jewish men (a minyan) to perform an exorcism.

Zitorsky: How about Milsky the butcher?

Alper: Milsky wouldn't come. Ever since they gave the seat by the East Wall to Kornblum, Milsky said he wouldn't set foot in this synagogue again. Every synagogue I have ever belonged to, there have always been two kosher butchers who get

> into a fight over who gets the favored seat
> by the East Wall during the High Holy
> Days, and the one who doesn't abandon
> the congregation in a fury, and the one
> who does always seems to die before the
> next High Holy Days.
>
> Schlissel: Kornblum the butcher died? I didn't
> know Kornblum died.
>
> Alper: Sure. Kornblum died four years ago.
>
> Schlissel: Well, he had lousy meat, believe me,
> may his soul rest in peace.

Paddy Chayefsky's *The Tenth Man* debuted at
the Booth Theatre in New York City in 1959.

AND WE SHALL SPREAD OUR VOICES AND SYMBOLS IN THIS NEW LAND

The Continental Congress assigned Thomas
Jefferson, Benjamin Franklin, and John Adams the
task of creating a great seal. Among the suggestions
in Jefferson's papers was a depiction of the Israelites
and Moses on the shore while Pharaoh and his army
drown in the Red Sea with the phrase, "Rebellion
to tyrants is obedience to God." Although this was
not adopted, some scholars speculate a connection
to Jewish numerology, in the eventual seal, because
the Hebrew letters in *echad* ("one," for God) add
up to thirteen, the number of arrows and leaves in
the eagle's talons, symbolizing the thirteen original
states and the tribes of ancient Israel.

Most could deduce that place names like
Jordan, Canaan, and Bethlehem derive from the
Hebrew Bible. Less well-known is that Salem, in
Massachusetts and Oregon, was a transliteration
from the Hebrew Shalom (peace). Important
Jewish people who were honored with "wheres"
include Noah, Tennessee, and Moses, New Mexico,
among others.

• • • ● • •

If the language spoken in Eastern European
Jewish homes was Yiddish, Hebrew, along with
Aramaic, is the language of religious ceremony and
prayer (also the official language of Israel). But
Hebrew was also important to the Puritans and
American scholars. When Harvard was founded,
students were required to study Hebrew one day a
week for three years. Preparation for the ministry
required the ability to read the Jewish scriptures in
the original Hebrew. Yale, Columbia, Brown, and
Princeton, among others, offered Hebrew courses
as well.

• • • ● • •

Inscribed on the Liberty Bell which tolled freedom for the country for the first time on July 8,
1776, are words from the Hebrew scriptures:
"Proclaim liberty throughout the land unto all the
inhabitants thereof."

CHERISHED MYTHS AND FACT

The six-pointed Star of David (the Jewish Star) was not generally a historic symbol for ancient Jews. The association started about two hundred years ago and was solidified as late as 1897, when Theodor Herzl's Zionist conference chose it as the symbol of the movement. The six-pointed star was used in some ancient Jewish contexts but can also be found in other religions, for instance, in a twelve-hundred-year-old Moslem mosaic floor near Tel Aviv.

• • • ● • •

The menorah, or seven-branched candelabrum *is* a historic Jewish symbol, found with great frequency on Jewish catacombs as far back as two thousand years.

• • • ● • •

The Bar Mitzvah ceremony, so emphasized by families and synagogues (and caterers), is not mentioned in the Bible. The ceremony merely emphasizes that at the age of thirteen years and one day, according to Jewish law, a child becomes a responsible adult within the religion and is required and privileged to read the Torah. The festivities and ceremony are only about five hundred years old. So a Jewish boy can be considered an adult without the ceremony.

Modern Israel was not the first to adopt Judaism as its state religion. A Turkic people, the Khazars, who migrated from Asia to Russia in the eighth century, adopted Judaism in a kingdom on the Volga River, and its ruling class spoke Hebrew. The kingdom was destroyed two centuries later by invaders from Kiev. It is thought they may have turned to Judaism to maintain neutrality in wars between Muslims and Christians.

A REMARKABLE PRESERVATION

Since ancient times Jews have scrupulously ensured the sanctity and validity of the Torah (the five books of Moses). These scrolls must be handwritten on fifty-seven parchments sewn together, a specific number of columns per sheet, letters per line, words per section. If even a small part of a letter is wrong, the entire scroll is unusable until corrected. No letter may be tampered with or deleted. A two-thousand-year-old scroll of the Book of Isaiah (part of the Dead Sea Scrolls) was found to have wording virtually identical to that of the book used today.

Good *Yontiff*!
(Happy Holidays)

My Jewishness informs my entire life. I do
the rituals and the holidays, and I love my
Jewishness. I love the tradition—the comfort
that I feel through the ancestral links of
centuries.

—MANDY PATINKIN

FREDDIE ROMAN'S FAVORITE JEWISH JOKE

More precisely, the author's favorite Freddie
Roman Jewish joke. When he told it during
the Broadway run of his hit show, *Catskills on
Broadway,* I was rolling in the aisles with such force
I dropped the brisket I was saving in my pocket for
intermission. Freddie was kind enough to retell it
for us now.

Those of you out here tonight of the Christian
faith, you are so lucky. Every year, December
25 is Christmas. Every year, exactly the same.
You could make plans!
    The Jewish people are not that lucky. We
have no idea where our holidays are. If we

don't have the Manischewitz Seven-Year
Calendar, we have no clue.

For example, our holiest day, is Yom
Kippur—or, as the Reformed Jew likes to say,
Yom Kip-pour (all our Reformed Rabbis like to
think they're Shakespeare).

Well, three years ago Yom Kippur came out
on October 27, which made Yom Kippur that
year very late.

And there isn't a Jew in this room tonight
that didn't say last year, 'You know,
Hannukah's early.'

You see, Jewish holidays are either late or
early. We are never on time.

· · · ● · ·

*Jewish holidays—believe it or not—do fall on the
same date every year. But only if you use the Jewish
calendar, which is based upon the 354- or 355-day
lunar year, as opposed to the 365- or 366-day
Gregorian solar year. So, to synchronize the dates with
the heavens, every nineteen years one month is added
seven times. Farshtaist? (Understand? Okay, we don't
either.) But we do know there are fifty-three holidays
and festivals in the Jewish year.*

· · · ● · ·

It's the night before Rosh Hashanah and the congregants are *shmoozing* (chatting) before services when a new member enters with a Saint Bernard.

"What chutzpah!" they whisper aloud.

Services begin, and all are amazed at how well the dog behaves—even wearing his own little prayer shawl and yarmulke.

The next morning the dog is seen swaying back and forth during prayers.

The following week, at the solemn Kol Nidre service for Yom Kippur, as the prayers begin, he stands on his hind legs and howls, "Ba-Roooooch!" more melodically even than the cantor.

Afterward everyone is clamoring to meet this man and his remarkable dog. Finally, the Rabbi says, "That's one talented pooch. You should really consider sending him to Rabbinical School."

The man shakes his head in disgust. "*You* talk to him! He wants to be a dentist."

• • ● • •

SHANA TOVAH! (HAPPY NEW YEAR!)

It's time to put your hand in the hand of someone you love . . . and recognize that we only have a very short opportunity to be the humans upon the sand and not the pebbles. . . . It's time to recognize that the real value of our lives is . . . experiencing the . . . seemingly insignificant things. It's time to recognize that things don't need to be the slickest . . . to be great . . . and appreciated. It's time to repent but not wallow in repentance. . . . It's time to take a stand for . . . what we believe. . . . It's time to realize that we are as small and as very large as the pebble upon the sand, no matter how we count the years. Amen.

—RABBI NEIL COMESS-DANIELS,
from his Rosh Hashanah sermon, 2000

ON THE HORNS OF A THOUGHTLESS ANIMAL

Jews blow the Shofar (ram's horn) on Rosh Hashanah (Jewish New Year) to remind us that through truth we can escape from our animalistic actions, which cause us to sin. The Shofar, which sounds like a trumpet wail, is much like the heart. Just as the heart is embedded in the narrow depths of the body, the Shofar is blown from the narrowest, lowest end—from the depths. A total of one-hundred notes are sounded each day. There are four types: *tekiah* (three seconds), *shevarim* (three one-second notes rising in tone), *teruah* (staccato notes extending for three seconds), and *tekiah gedolah* (a final blast in a set that lasts as long as the Shofar can blow).

Throughout my life, when I was moving further and further from Judaism, I always clung to a single thread—Yom Kippur. On that one day I fasted. I might be shooting it out with Burt Lancaster or John Wayne, or battling Laurence Olivier and his Romans (*Spartacus*) . . . but I always fasted. . . . And let me tell you, it's not easy making love to Ava Gardner on an empty stomach.

—KIRK DOUGLAS

Douglas, born Issur Danielovitch, the son of Russian immigrants, returned to his roots, reaffirming his commitment to Judaism with a second Bar Mitzvah—on his eighty-third birthday.

• • • ● • • •

Fish and Lipper have been feuding for years. On Yom Kippur (Day of Atonement) Eve, the Rabbi brings the two men together and asks them to make peace.

"After all," says the Rabbi, "what is the point of going into synagogue and asking G-d to forgive you when you can't even forgive each other?"

The men, moved, hug and promise not to fight anymore. At the end of services, Fish makes a beeline for Lipper.

"Lipper, I want you to know, I prayed for you everything you prayed for me."

"Ahha!" says Lipper. "Starting up already?"

IS THERE A WRITER IN THE HOUSE?

On a particular night after Yom Kippur, Jay Leno encountered dead silence after delivering his monologue on *The Tonight Show*. Thinking fast, he quipped in an aside, "It's tough to get good jokes written during a Jewish holiday."

—Courtesy of JAY LENO

• • • • • • •

'TWAS THE NIGHT BEFORE HANNUKAH
(FESTIVAL OF LIGHTS)

'Twas the night before Hannukah, as it is said;
   And Santa was sitting and hocking his head;

He had all the toys wrapped up nice in his
   zeckel; For *maidlach* and boys to give each
   one a *peckel*.

The reindeer were saddled and ready to fly;
   Like a crew of brave astronauts all through
   the sky;

But Santa was starving to eat a good *meichel*;
   Some delicious food that would stick to his
   beichel.

Not plum cakes or mincemeat or peppermint
   candy; But some Kosher cooking he
   thought would be dandy;

So he called to his reindeer, "Hey *kinder*, To a
   Jewish *balbusta* we go and don't be so
   slow."

The house had no chimney, so he went
   through the door, And kissed the *mezzuzah*
   and jumped on the floor;

Then the man of the house smiled. "Santa, you
   devil, Come in, don't be shy, and see our
   split level.

"The night is still early, there's plenty of *zeit*,
    So come in the den and please have a bite;

If only we knew you were coming, by gosh,
    But I'll call out the wife and she'll give you
    a nosh.

A slice of stuffed derma, a few little strudels,
    Some chicken, chopped liver, some *flanken*
    with noodles;

Some *blintzes*, some *kreplach*, some lox and
    bialy, A *bissel* chopped herring, an end piece
    of challah.

"And if all of these goodies don't fill up your
    gatkes, Last but not least, some Hannukah
    latkes.

"A latke?" cried Santa, "what is this delight?
    On the outside it's golden and inside it's
    white.

On top it's so crisp and inside it's yummy," So
    he gobbled them up till he filled his *groisseh*
    tummy.

Then they gave him a dreidel and showed him
    the plays, And he took a Menorah to light
    for eight days;

And to give Santa the spirit and to show how
    they felt, For *mazel* they gave him some
    Hannukah *gelt*.

He beamed and he chuckled and said, "*Kine-ahora*, I don't want to feel like a Hannukah *shnorrer*.

To show you how much I enjoyed your snack, I'm leaving some goodies I've shlepped in my sack."

Then he called to his reindeer and said, "*Luz mir gehn*." And each one obeyed as he shlepped on the rein.

"Giddyap, Irving, hoo ha, Sidney,

Hi-ho, Sadie, let's go, Minnie,

Onward, Gussie, upward, Solly,

So nu, Becky, oy vay, Molly!"

And they swore that he yelled as he rode out of sight:

"Merry latkes to all—and to all a good night."

BRIEF TRANSLATIONS:

zeckel (bag); *maidlach* (girls); *peckel* (coin); *meichel* (meal); *beichel* (stomach); *kinder* (children); *balbusta* (good housewife); *mezzuzah* (portion of Deuteronomy in an ornament); *zeit* (time); *flanken* (flank steak); *blintzes* (rolled pancakes); *kreplach* (filled noodles); *bissel* (little); *gatkes* (long underwear); *latkes* (potato pancakes); *groisseh* (big);

mazel (luck); *gelt* (money); *Kine-ahora* (No evil eye!); *shnorrer* (taker); *Luz mir gehn* (Let me go).

Short summary of every Jewish holiday: "They tried to kill us, we won, let's eat."

A LITTLE JOY

Can you guess, children, which is the best
of all holidays? Hannukah, of course. . . .
Mother is in the kitchen rendering goose fat
and frying pancakes. . . . You eat pancakes
every day."

—SHALOM ALEICHEM

A LITTLE OY

Arkady was the only Jew I ever shared a cell
with in the gulag. We celebrated Hannukah
together in Chistopol prison in 1980, lighting
pieces of wax paper we had stashed away for
months and hoping they would last long
enough for us to say prayers over them.

—NATAN (ANATOLY) SHARANSKY
(Russian refusenik and author, and
Israeli political leader)

I believe that as a Jew and a human being I have an ethical imperative to look at any circumstance that deprives people of their liberty. That's what fuels me. That's why I write the songs, why I sing the songs.

—PETER YARROW,
Peter, Paul, and Mary,
Hadassah magazine, November 1994

[On Purim, Feast of Lots] one need send "potions [gifts]" to only one friend or neighbor, but must give gifts to at least two poor persons. . . . It is better to lavish gifts on the poor than to feast heavily or give presents to your friends. For there is no greater joy than bringing gladness to the poor, the orphan, the widow, and all those who have no kin.

—MOSES MAIMONIDES (1135–1204,
Spanish Rabbi, physician, scholar,
philosopher, author),
Hilchot Megilla (2:16–17)

• • • ● • • •

Passover [Feast of Unleavened Bread] is the most meaningful holiday to me, and I spend it with my family. . . . There is a Jewish tradition of show business which has influenced my career. My Jewishness has made my outlook on life more ironic and earnest.

—WENDY WASSERSTEIN
(playwright)

A man visits his Rabbi.

"Rabbi," he says. "I raised my son to be a good Jew, taught him the Torah, instructed him about the Sabbath. Well, I learned at this last Passover that he converted. Tell me, what I should do!"

The Rabbi says, "The exact same thing happened to my son. I taught him to follow in my footsteps and boom! He also converted—and became a priest! I don't know what to tell you. Maybe we should ask G-d?"

The two men start praying: "G-d almighty, Creator of the Universe, we are at a loss. Our firstborn sons have converted. What should we do?"

A thundering voice responds: "*Well, tell me about it!*"

Passover has a message for the conscience and the heart of all mankind. For what does it commemorate? It commemorates the deliverance of a people from degrading slavery, from most foul and cruel tyranny. And so, it is Israel's—nay, G-d's—protest against unrighteousness, whether individual or national. Wrong, it declares, may triumph for a time, but even though it be perpetrated by the strong on the weak, it will meet with its inevitable retribution at last.

—MORRIS JOSEPH (1848–1930, British Reform Rabbi, theologian), Judaism as Creed and Life

Oy, Mamma Mia! The basis for pizza is none other than—matzah. Jewish unleavened Passover bread. It seems that about two thousand years ago Roman soldiers added a little olive and cheese. (The pepperoni came later.)

• • • ● • • •

My husband, an English Jew, tells the following joke—each and every Passover—to all, including strangers on subways—and Easter bunnies. (Don't ask!)

An English Jew is about to be knighted. The queen's protocol officer explains he is to recite certain Latin words.

On the day of the ceremony, the poor man is so nervous that when he approaches the queen, he forgets the Latin. As she stands tapping her foot, he suddenly bursts out with "Ma nish-ta-na ha-laila hazeh mi-kol ha-leilot?"*

Completely confused, the queen turns to her protocol officer, shakes her head, and whispers, "Why is this knight different from all other knights?"

---

*One of the four questions asked by the youngest at the Passover Seder: "Why is this night different from all other nights?"

• • • ● • •

The Depression shattered Weinstein's Uncle
Meyer, who kept his fortune under the mat-
tress. When the market crashed, the government called in all mattresses, and Meyer
became a pauper overnight. All that was left
for him was to jump out the window sill of
the Flatiron Building from 1930 to 1937.

"These kids with their pot and their sex,"
Uncle Meyer was fond of saying. "Do they
know what it is to sit on a window sill for
seven years? There you see life! Of course,
everybody looks like ants. But each year
Tessie—may she rest in peace—made the
Seder right out there on the ledge. The family
gathered round for Passover. Oy, nephew!
What's the world coming to when they have a
bomb that can kill more people than one look
at Max Rifkin's daughter?"

—WOODY ALLEN,
"No Kaddish for Weinstein"

• • • ● • • •

If I fail to protect your freedom, your
dignity, I have failed to protect my own.
And . . . there is no higher standard, no
more precious obligation, than protecting
everyone's right to be who we are, in peace.

—THE AUTHOR
in *Ask Sadie,* Christmas, 2000

We must refuse to let it make sense—here, or
anywhere else. We must steel ourselves against
rationalizations and learned political analysis.
We must hang on, as long as possible, to our
sense of astonishment. Be astonished that ide-
ology can make murder understandable. Be
astonished that hatred can go unchecked until
bodies burn. Let us not be misled by labels, as
if calling someone a terrorist gives sense to
madness.

—RABBI DAN SHEVITZ
of Emanuel Synagogue,
Oklahoma City as part of his
sermon on the final day of Passover,
three days after the April 19, 1995
bombing of the Alfred P. Murrah
Federal Building

ON SHAVUOT THE RABBI GOLFED LATE!

The rabbi was an avid golfer. If he didn't play he would get withdrawal symptoms. One Shavuot (Feast of Harvest) the Rabbi thought to himself, "What's it going to hurt if I take a little recess from all-night prayer and play a few rounds?" Sure enough, the Rabbi snuck out of the synagogue and headed straight for the golf course. Looking down were Moses and G-d.

Moses said, "Look how terrible—a Rabbi on Shavuot!"

G-d replied, "Watch, I'm going to teach him a lesson."

The Rabbi stepped up to the first tee. When he hit the ball, it careened off a tree, struck a rock, skipped across a pond, and landed—for a hole in one!

Moses protested: "G-d, this is how you teach him a lesson? By giving him a hole in one?"

"Ah," said G-d, "but who's he going to tell?"

And you shall call the Sabbath a delight.
—ISAIAH (58:13)

I shall never forget Shabbat in my town.
When I shall have forgotten everything else,
my memory will still retain the atmosphere of
holiday, of serenity pervading even the poor-
est houses; the white tablecloth, the candles,
the meticulously combed little girls, the men
on their way to the synagogue.

—ELIE WIESEL
(Romanian-born author,
professor, and survivor,
dedicated to preserving the
memory of the Holocaust)

Considering the suffering that pervades the
whole historical life of the Jew, it is surely
a wonder that he could continually maintain such equanimity, such genuine humor,
without which he would never have been
able to lift himself again and again from
the deepest humiliation to proud heights.
The Jewish holidays have brought about
this wonder for him.

—HERMANN COHEN
(German philosopher, 1842–1918)

... Choose Somebody Else for a Change?*

My father, Louis Winston, may he rest in peace, loved telling this story about being in the army overseas during World War II—and being Jewish.

In 1943, while stationed in Burma, he went into a local bar. He ordered a beer and, lo and behold, a very inebriated Australian weaved over to him.

Heavy glass in hand, he spat. "Hey—you a Yid?"**

Here we go again, thought my father, getting off the stool—at the ready. "Yeah! What about it!"

Suddenly the Australian jumped back. "Now, don't get hexited, mate! Don't get hexited! It tykes a Yid to know a Yid."

---

*The end of a classic joke that starts "G-d, if we are the Chosen People, would you please . . ."
**An offensive word for a Jew when pronounced as in *id* with a *y*. Not offensive when pronounced "Yeed."

I think my father enjoyed this story so because the "here we go again" turned into a punch line—instead of something altogether different and altogether too familiar.

And, yes, even for the rich and the famous not so very long ago . . .

Since my little son is only half-Jewish, would it be all right if he went into the pool only up to his waist?

—GROUCHO MARX,
addressing a country club
that would not admit his son

Yes, I am a Jew, and when the ancestors of the right honourable gentleman were brutal savages in an unknown island, mine were priests in the Temple of Solomon.

—BENJAMIN DISRAELI,
replying to a taunt that he was
descended from "miscreant" Jews

• • • ● • • •

When I was thrown out of college, I got a job
on Madison Avenue in New York. A real
dyed-in-the-wool advertising agency on
Madison Avenue wanted a man to come in
and they'd pay him ninety-five dollars a week
to sit in their office and look Jewish. They
wanted to prove to the outside world that
they would hire minority groups, you know.
So I was the one they hired. I was the show
Jew with the agency. I tried to look Jewish
desperately. Used to read my memos from
right to left all the time. They fired me finally
because I took off too many Jewish holidays.

—WOODY ALLEN, part of a longer
"Love Story" monologue recorded at
Mr. Kelly's in Chicago, March 1964,
and released on *Woody Allen*
(Colpix, 1964)

• • • ● • • •

> *Now that the world is wracked by peace, people can go back to what they love best: anti-Semitism.*
>
> —MORT SAHL

You don't have to like Jews but for those of you who don't . . .

> I suggest you boycott certain Jewish products: the Wassermann test for syphilis; Digitalis, discovered by Dr. Nuslin; Insulin, discovered by Dr. Minofsky; Chloralhydrate for convulsions, discovered by Dr. Casimir Funk; Streptomycin, discovered by Dr. Selman Waksman; the Polio pill by Dr. Albert Sabin, and the . . . vaccine by Dr. Jonas Salk."
>
> —SAM LEVINSON

> The Trotskys make the revolutions and the Bronsteins pay the bills.
>
> —RABBI JACOB MAZE,
> a 1921 comment about Leon Trotsky,
> who was born Lev Bronstein

Frankfort, 1788. Mayer (Papa) Rothschild's shop. A pogrom is around them. The family is headed to the cellar. Only twelve-year-old Nathan remains above—with Papa.

Mayer: Quick! . . . Downstairs! Hurry!
    Nathan . . . I told you to go downstairs.

Nathan (bitterly): Papa—I hate them.

Mayer: Don't ever say that.

Nathan: But they hate us.

Mayer: What's that got to do with us? They're a mob. We're a family. Hatred comes cheap to a mob. A family buys it dear.

—*The Rothschilds*, Act 1, Scene 6
(Provided by MTI)

From these roots, the House of Rothschild remains two hundred years later. What was handed down from father to son became one of the richest, most honored financial dynasties in Europe.

The Rothschilds, the musical play, music by Jerry Bock, lyrics by Sheldon Harnick, book by Sherman Yellen, based on Frederic Morton's *The Rothschilds*, opened on Broadway in 1970. (The author's son and assistant on this project, Simon Winston-Macauley, played young Nathan during the summer of 1990 in the Circle on the Square Revival, bringing *nakhes* to his parents—and everyone they ever met.)

Strange and
Wonderful Bedfellows

Throughout history a number of religious and world leaders, scholars, and not-so-ordinary men and women, though not Jewish themselves, have rallied in support of the Jewish people—sometimes risking their lives. In some cases they were great. In others greatness was thrust upon them. But here are some of our strange and wonderful bedfellows.

• • • ● ● • •

After the destruction of the First Temple 2,500 years ago, the Persian king, Cyrus II, defeated the Babylonians, permitted the Jews to return to the Land of Israel, and encouraged them to rebuild the Temple—a feat that took only seventy years.

• • • ● ● • •

Alexander the Great (356–323 B.C.E.)—allowed Palestine to flourish and helped create a great Jewish community in the ancient world's Alexandria.

Julius Caesar (100–44 B.C.E.) granted Jews full religious freedoms, including exempting them from military service in accordance with laws regarding the Sabbath and kosher food, and recognizing special Jewish courts to handle problems of the Jewish community. Caesar's heirs continued his generosity.

The Roman emperors Elagabalus (204–222 C.E.) and Severus Alexander (208–235), unlike some of their predecessors, were so enamored of Judaism that the former eschewed pork and was circumcised and the latter's enemies referred to him with terms approximating *Rabbi*.

Julian (331–363), the last pagan Roman Emperor, was highly pro-Jewish, abolishing extra taxes and informing the Jewish community in writing of his intention to rebuild Jerusalem for Jews.

• • • ● • •

While Napoleon (1769–1821) enacted some restrictive measures against Jews, he proved relatively enlightened for his time: In 1799 he issued a proclamation urging restoring a Jewish homeland in Palestine; in 1808 he established a central Jewish communal administration. More, he extended civil rights to Jews in France, Germany and Italy, laying the groundwork for full emancipation in Europe in the nineteenth century.

• • • ● • •

Christian Publishing Allies: From the sixteenth through nineteenth centuries, some of the most important forces in the spread of Jewish learning were Christian.

Daniel Bomberg, a Venetian Christian printer, took great care to print the Talmud (around 1520) and continued publishing a large range of Jewish material (over two hundred works). He was the first to print the rabbinic Bible and introduced innovations (adding chapter numbers in Hebrew) that influenced future Bibles.

Other non-Jews who wrote sympathetically and extensively about the history of the Jews were a French Protestant pastor, Jacques Basnage (1653–1725), who wrote in Rotterdam, and Hannah Adams (1755–1831), the first professional woman writer in America.

A HOLY BROTHERHOOD

A number of Popes have been important allies and supporters of Jews and Jewish culture. Notably, Popes Gregory I (540–604) and Gregory X (1210–1276), both of whom defended the Jews by philosophy and decree against attack. And, in a most courageous act of enlightenment, Pope Leo X (1475–1521) encouraged the first printing of the complete Talmud (fifteen volumes) in Venice around 1520; this was a highly significant event during a period when Talmud manuscripts were intermittently burned and the work's teaching was forbidden.

HE WHO SAVES A SINGLE LIFE SAVES THE ENTIRE WORLD (TALMUDIC VERSE)

The unsung hero Varian Fry, a non-Jewish editor from New York City who was born in 1907 and died in obscurity in 1967, has finally been recognized as having helped thousands of artists in the Vichy French zone escape Nazi terror during World War II. Despite having no training in underground techniques, he was part of a mission that saved, among countless others, Max Ernst, Marc Chagall, André Breton and Jacques Lipchitz. In 1991, fifty years after his courageous action and twenty-four years after his death, the man called the American Schindler received his first official recognition from the U.S. Holocaust Memorial Council. In 1996 he was the first American to be named "Righteous Among the Nations" by the Holocaust Heroes and Martyrs Remembrance Authority in Jerusalem, and *Guinness World Records 2001* notes his achievement as a record for saving artists. In recent years the popular media, notably in England and in the United States, have made films and programs detailing his remarkable achievements on behalf of Jews.

HE WHO SAVES A SINGLE LIFE SAVES THE ENTIRE WORLD (TALMUDIC VERSE)

"For me there's no choice. I've taken this assignment, and I'd never be able to go back to Stockholm without knowing inside myself I'd done all a man could do to save as many Jews as possible." So said Raoul Wallenberg, the Swede, who though he contained only a drop of Jewish blood, through formal (and informal) channels issued Swedish passports (Schutz-Passes or Wallenberg passports) during the Holocaust, operated "Swedish Houses" in Pest, jumped atop trains to camps, and interrupted death marches to save over 100,000 Jews.

He disappeared in 1945. Finally, in November 2000, the Russians reported that he had been executed in the Lubyanka Headquarters of the NKVD (later the KGB). For his heroism, Wallenberg was made an honorary citizen of the United States (1981), Canada (1985), and Israel (1986).

HE WHO SAVES A SINGLE LIFE SAVES THE ENTIRE WORLD (TALMUDIC VERSE)

"Having a son, I felt, as a German, I should act." These were the words of Beate Klarsfeld. The daughter of a German soldier and goddaughter of a Nazi official, she became a Nazi hunter after marrying a Jew, Serge Klarsfeld, in Paris when she was twenty-one. After hearing the atrocities committed against his family, and following the election of a Nazi propagandist as chancellor of Germany in 1968, she felt the younger generation of Germans should not tolerate this—and slapped the leader in the face at a rally, making her a famous activist. In 1972 the couple discovered that the notorious Nazi Klaus Barbie was hiding in Bolivia, and they spend the next eleven years trying to bring him to justice, succeeding in 1983, when he was deported to France, found guilty of crimes against humanity, and sentenced to life imprisonment.

• • • ● • • •

HE WHO SAVES A SINGLE LIFE SAVES THE ENTIRE WORLD (TALMUDIC VERSE)

We won. We're here. We had children, and they gave us grandchildren, and I stand here and say to myself, "It's 1994 and you're here, alive." Who would believe it?

—HENRIK LICHTENSON,
a Schindler survivor, at a screening of
Steven Spielberg's *Schindler's List*

I re-emerged [to Judaism] . . . through the birth of my children and through a decision . . . about how I was going to raise them. . . . I think that's what led me, that and events around the world, very naturally and . . . in a very smooth way . . . to make *Schindler's List*.

—STEVEN SPIELBERG

• • ● • •

> She . . . went to a china closet. . . . She
> brought out a wad of money—Occupation
> Zloty.
>
> "I have a sister. . . . I want you to spend this
> buying her back if ever she's put in the cattle
> cars. . . ."
>
> " . . . How much is it?"
>
> "Four thousand zloty."
>
> He took it . . . her nest egg. . . . It was still
> safer with him than . . . . behind the closet. . . .
>
> Helen Hirsch would never see her 4,000
> zloty again—not in a form in which they could
> be . . . held in the hand. But to this day she
> considers it a matter of small importance that
> Oskar Schindler was so inexact with sums of
> money.
>
> —THOMAS KENEALLY,
> *Schindler's List*

When the Czech-born ethnic German Catholic
whose "list" saved countless Jews from the concentration camps died on October 9, 1974, his remains
were taken to Israel, where his lead coffin was carried through the streets of Jerusalem. He was
buried in the Catholic churchyard on Mount Zion
in the presence of hundreds of weeping Schindler
Jews.

Oskar Schindler was mourned on four continents.

Mountains of Moments

> Just as there are mountains in space, there are mountains in time. Just as there are high places, so are there high moments. . . . We can and do make mountains out of moments.
>
> —RABBI SIDNEY GREENBERG

"SOMETHING IS ONLY DANGEROUS IF YOU ARE NOT PREPARED FOR IT"

So said Dr. Judith Resnik, who was determined to become the second American woman in space. The Ohio native obtained perfect SAT scores; she was a gourmet cook and a classical pianist who commented, "I never play anything softly."

The woman with a doctorate in electrical engineering was selected as an astronaut candidate by NASA in 1978. Her maiden voyage was on the space shuttle *Discovery*.

Millions saw her on television as she boarded the *Challenger* on January 28, 1986, at 11:38 A.M. EST. She was carrying a ring for her nephew and a locket for her niece.

At 11:39, just seconds after launch, the *Challenger* exploded.

Dr. Judith Resnik was thirty-seven years old.

If you do not let your son grow up as a Jew, you deprive him of those sources of energy which cannot be replaced by anything else. He will have to struggle as a Jew. . . . Do not deprive him of that advantage.

—SIGMUND FREUD

It is change, continuing change, inevitable change, that is the dominant factor in society today. No sensible decision can be made any longer without taking into account not only the world as it is, but the world as it will be.

—ISAAC ASIMOV

I believe with complete faith that within the human race there are prophets, individuals of outstanding merit and great intellect, from whom prophesy emanates.

—MOSES MAIMONIDES

The vaccine works!

—Announced by a young researcher, JONAS SALK, on April 12, 1955

By Us, He's an Einstein

If my theory of relativity is proven successful, Germany will claim me as a German and France will declare that I am a citizen of the world. Should my theory prove untrue, France will say that I am a German, and Germany will declare that I am a Jew.

The Jew who abandons his faith . . . is in a position similar to a snail that abandons its shell. He remains a Jew.

Only when we [Jews] have the courage to regard ourselves as a nation, only when we have respect for ourselves, can we win the respect of others.

—Albert Einstein

In 1952 Albert Einstein was offered the presidency of Israel. Though he declined, upon his death on April 18, 1955, he left his manuscripts and royalties to Hebrew University.

> ## "GIVE ME YOUR TIRED, YOUR POOR, YOUR HUDDL'D MASSES YEARNING TO BREATHE FREE"

Most of us recognize this great American quotation as inscribed on the Statue of Liberty. It was written as part of the poem "The New Colossus" by Emma Lazarus. Lazarus, a poet and activist, was also founder of the Society for the Improvement and Colonization of East European Jews and one of the founders of the Zionist movement. Her place in the history of the statue is sealed forever.

Donated by France, the statue sat in pieces for several years awaiting funds to build the base and assemble "her." In 1883 an auction was held. Though Walt Whitman and Mark Twain contributed manuscripts, the highest bid, fifteen hundred dollars, was received for "The New Colossus," written by the young Lazarus a few days after her return from Europe, where she saw the persecution of Jews firsthand.

It was not until 1888 that Lady Liberty assumed her place in New York Harbor. Sadly, Emma Lazarus did not live to witness this historic event, having died a year earlier at the age of thirty-eight.

Her words, however, were so inspiring that they were inscribed on a tablet inside the statue in 1903. "The New Colossus" became an immortal expression of hope for the new immigrant.

The grammar schools of the Jewish quarter
are overcrowdeed with children of immigrants.
. . . The poor laborer . . . will pinch himself
to keep his child at college, rather than send
him to factory to contribute to the family's
income.

—ABRAHAM CAHAN,
in the *Atlantic Monthly,* July 1898

Judaism has always insisted that knowledge
has the power not only to make people smart
but to make them good.

—RABBI HAROLD KUSHNER

If I were a Rothschild, I'd be richer than
Rothschild. First of all, I'd have all
Rothschild's money, and then I'd make a little
bit on the side as a tailor.

—SHOLEM ALEICHEM

"THE ANGEL OF DEATH NEVER ASKS IF THE SHROUD IS READY"

These were the words of Sholem Aleichem, born
Solomon Rabinowitz in Russia in 1859, who was
known as the Yiddish Mark Twain. Some of his
works were the basis for *Fiddler on the Roof*. He
died at age fifty-seven on May 13, 1916, in a
shabby Bronx apartment. Because he always num-
bered page 13 page 12a, every May 12a has been
observed as the anniversary of his death.

His granddaughter, the noted writer and lec-
turer Bel Kaufman, has said that his will stipulated:
"Preserve your *Yiddishkeit* [Jewish beliefs]. I don't
want any monuments. If people read my books,
that will be my best monument." She noted that in
later years people read her grandfather's will with
great feeling. "That first year, the . . . Yiddish poet
Nochum Yud . . . slowed down when he came to
the line 'Take good care of your mother. Sweeten
her life.' And I saw the tears in my grandmother's
eyes."

On Aleichem's tombstone is inscribed: "*Daw ligt a Yid, a poshuter, Geshribn Yiddish-Deitsch far vaiber. Un far 'n prosten folk hawt er; Geven a humorist, a shreiber*" [Here lies a simple Jew who wrote in Jewish-German for women. For plain folks he was a humorist and writer]."

His will further stipulated, "Bury me among the poor, that my grave may shine on theirs and their graves on mine."

What is hateful unto you, don't do unto your neighbor. The rest is commentary.

—RABBI HILLEL

Without Them,
WOULD THIS WORLD BE QUITE SO WISE?

Barbara Walters   WALTER ANNENBERG

Irving R. Levine

ABRAHAM CAHAN

CARL BERNSTEIN   Joseph Pulitzer

Larry King

ARTHUR M. SCHLESINGER

A. M. Rosenthal

ARTHUR SULZBERGER

MARVIN KALB   *Walter Lippmann*

Samuel Irving Newhouse

Mike Wallace   Nat Hentoff

Meyer Berger   *Wolfe Blitzer*

Elie Abel   **Ted Koppel**

Jeff Greenfield

David Halberstam

Sydney Schanberg

DANIEL SCHORR   *Edwin Newman*

I. F. Stone   *William Safire*

MORLEY SAFER   **SEYMOUR HERSH**

Adolph Ochs

MILTON FRIEDMAN

Paul Samuelson

Leonard Lyons   **Theodore H. White**

Baron Paul von Reuter

Daniel Boorstin   **BARBARA TUCHMAN**

Bob Simon   **Annie Nathan Meyer**

Rabbi Joseph Telushkin

JOE ROSENTHAL

Art Buchwald   **Ruth Westheimer**

*All have at least one Jewish parent.

"The truth has many faces" (Yiddish Proverb)

ATTENTION MUST BE PAID

> Linda Loman: I don't say he's a great man. Willy Loman never made a lot of money. His name was never in the paper. He's not the finest character that ever lived. But he's a human being, and a terrible thing is happening to him. So attention must be paid. He's not allowed to fall into his grave like a dog. Attention, attention must be finally paid to such a person.
>
> —ARTHUR MILLER,
> *Death of a Salesman*

Death of a Salesman premiered on Broadway on February 10, 1949, starring Lee J. Cobb. The Pulitzer Prize–winning play has won multiple Tonys from its first run through its highly successful revivals.

• • • ● • • •

DIVINE ANDROGYNY OF THE SOUL

> She wasn't cut out for a woman's life. She couldn't sew, she couldn't knit. She let the food burn and the milk boil over; her Sabbath pudding never turned out right, and her challah dough didn't rise. . . . Her father . . . had studied the Torah with his daughter as if she were a son. He told [her] to lock the doors and drape the window."
>
> —ISAAC BASHEVIS SINGER,
> "Yentl, the Yeshiva Boy"

Androgyny of the soul is the subject of Isaac Bashevis Singer's "Yentl," the tale, the 1975 Broadway play, and the 1984 Barbra Streisand film. In each the premise—a young woman forced to disguise herself as a boy because she longed to study Judaism when such pursuits were reserved for males—is constant. In the film, however, Streisand plays out Yentl's struggle differently, exploring "Where is it written?"

• • ● • •

SISTERHOOD

A FIFTY-FOURTH BIRTHDAY. THREE SISTERS,
DIVERSE IN THEIR ASSIMILATION YET BONDED IN
LOVE, REUNITE. THERE ARE RECRIMINATIONS,
LAUGHTER, ACCEPTANCE—AND UNEXPECTED
ROMANCE FOR THE EXPATRIATE, ATHEISTIC
SARA WITH MERVYN-THE-FURRIER—WHO IS
PERHAPS A LITTLE LESS UNLIKELY THAN SHE
IMAGINED.

1991

Sara: Your world is very different from mine.

Merv: No, it's not. I changed my name . . .
and my daughter, the Israeli captain, went
to Saint Paul's. . . . Sara, you're an American Jewish woman living in London, working for a Chinese Hong Kong bank . . .
with a daughter who's running off to
Lithuania!

Sara: And who are you? My knight in shining
armor? The furrier who came to dinner.
Why won't you give up, Merv? I'm a cold,
bitter woman who's turned her back on her
family, her religion, and her country! . . .

   You deserve someone who really does
know how to throw a good Shabbes.
Someone who will. . . . show up at holidays . . . in a . . . cheery crepe orange suit.

Merv: And you can't, Sara Rosensweig?

Sara: . . . Orange pales my already far too sallow skin.

Merv: (extends hand) It was a pleasure to meet you, Sara.

Sara: (holds onto his hand) You're a very nice man.

—WENDY WASSERSTEIN,
The Sisters Rosensweig

The Sisters Rosensweig opened at the Ethel Barrymore Theatre on March 18, 1993, and won the Outer Critics Circle Award.

A king of flesh and blood stamps his image on a coin, hence all coins look and are alike; but the King of Kings has stamped every man with the seal of the first man, yet no man is like any other.

—MISHNA 4:5

• • • ● • • •

Found in Yonkers . . .

Jay: I er . . . I just want to say thank you for taking us in, Grandma. I know it wasn't easy for you.

Grandma: Dot's right. It vasn't.

Jay: It wasn't easy for us either. But I think I learned a lot since I'm here. Some good and some bad. Do you know what I mean, Grandma?

Grandma: You're not afraid to say the truth. Dot's good. . . . You want to hear what my truth is? . . . Everything hurts. Whatever it is you get good in life, you also lose something.

Jay: I guess I'm too young to understand that.

Grandma: And I'm too old to forget it.

—NEIL SIMON'S
Lost in Yonkers

"It's not so important dat you hate me. . . . It's only important dat you live." So were Grandma's words in Neil Simon's *Lost in Yonkers,* the story of a family in 1942 whose matriarch, shaped by hardship and driven by survival, is forced to examine what she sacrificed—love. Winner of four Tony

Awards and the 1991 Pulitzer Prize, the play
opened February 21 at the Richard Rodgers
Theater.

Note: The author's son and assistant on this
project, Simon, was proud to be part of its cast
for a time. Now that's *kvelling* (beaming with
intense pride).

Without Them,
WOULD THIS WORLD BE QUITE AS HUMANE?

Bernard Baruch   SIMON WIESENTHAL

Herbert H. Lehman   STEPHEN WISE

HILLEL   SOLOMON SCHECHTER

Bella Abzug   Baruch Spinoza

Samuel Gompers   Golda Meir

Cyrus Adler   Elie Wiesel

Henrietta Szold   David Ben-Gurion

Menachem Schneerson

Benjamin Cardozo

Henry Kissinger   Theodor Herzl

MOSHE DAYAN   Anne Frank

Samuel Belkin   Menachem Begin

Jonathan Netanyahu   ROBERT BRISCOE

LOUIS D. BRANDEIS

Chaim Weizmann

ARTHUR GOLDBERG

Hyman Rickover   YITZHAK RABIN

Ernestine Louise Rose   **Maimonides**

Felix Frankfurter   HANNAH GREENBAUM SOLOMON

Naomi Wolf   *Jacob Schiff*

ISAAC WISE   SALLY PRIESAND

Ruth Bader Ginsburg

HENRY M. MORGENTHAU, JR.

Judah P. Benjamin   Abraham Ribicoff

Joseph Lieberman

David Dubinsky

Saul Alinsky   ADOLPHUS SIMEON SOLOMONS

Joel Springarn   **Judah Magnes**

Rebecca Gratz   *Louis Lipsky*

THE SEIXAS FAMILY

Oscar Solomon Straus   Avi Weiss

Abraham L. Sachar   **Benjamin Frankel**

FELIX WARBURG   RABBI HAROLD KUSHNER

Rabbi Abba Hillel Silver

---

*All have at least one Jewish parent.

293

"If you will it, it is no dream"
—Theodor Herzl

Our forefathers have been forced out of many, many places at a moment's notice. . . . Maybe that's why we always wear our hats.

—Fiddler on the Roof

Constable: I have an order . . . be out of here in three days. . . .

First Man: After a lifetime, a piece of paper and get thee out. . . .

Mendel: Rabbi, we've been waiting for the Messiah all our lives. Wouldn't this be a good time for him to come?

Rabbi: We'll have to wait for him someplace else. Meanwhile, let's start packing.

—Fiddler on the Roof,
based on Sholem Aleichem's stories, book by Joseph Stein

"THE HEART IS SMALL AND EMBRACES THE WHOLE WIDE WORLD" (JEWISH PROVERB)

1937. THE OVERBURDENED JEROME FAMILY ALREADY HAS THREE EXTRA MOUTHS TO FEED.

Stan: You really think there'll be a war, Pop? . . .

Pop: We're already in it. . . . If you're Jewish, you've got a cousin suffering *somewhere* in the world. . . .

Stan: How many relatives do we have in Europe?

Ma: Enough. Uncles, cousins. I have a great-aunt. Your father has nephews.

Pop: I have a cousin, Sholem, in Poland. His whole family. . .

Stan: What if they got to America? Where would they live?. . . Where would we put them? . . .

Pop: What God gives us to deal with, we deal with . . .

—NEIL SIMON,
Brighton Beach Memoirs

AND THERE WAS A YOUNG VOICE THAT COULD NEVER BE SILENCED . . .

It's really a wonder that I haven't dropped all my ideals. . . . Yet, I keep them, because in spite of everything, I still believe that people are really good at heart. . . . I can feel the sufferings of millions and yet, if I look up into the heavens, I think that it will all come right, that this cruelty too will end, and that peace and tranquility will return again. In the meantime, I must uphold my ideals, for perhaps the time will come when I shall be able to carry them out.

—ANNE FRANK
The Diary of a Young Girl
July 15, 1944

On August 4, 1944, the Gestapo found the hiding place of the Frank family. Seven months later, Anne Frank died in the Belsen concentration camp in Germany.

She was not yet fifteen.

• • ● ● • •

"My father was a Zionist. . . . In 1919 he worked directly with Chaim Weizmann at the Second Zionist Congress. . . . When I was fourteen . . . my father took us . . . up to the Waldorf-Astoria to meet Chaim Weizmann . . . the day before he went to Washington to persuade President Truman to recognize the State of Israel. Secret Servicemen escorted us into Weizmann's room. . . . I expected him to be . . . seventeen feet tall. So I was surprised to meet this little man who had spots on his bald head and was going blind. He asked me when I was going to Israel. "Next year if there's peace," I said because that's what I'd been told to say.

But he chastised me: "There will be peace." . . .

As we were leaving, Weizmann said to my father, *Tsvay feiner kinder*—two fine children. It was like George Washington telling your father, "Nice kids."

Whatever my father was or wasn't, he was a Zionist. He had a passion about it. . . . He sat at the kitchen table listening to the radio while the United Nations voted on partition.

They ticked off the names of the countries. When they got to Uruguay, which put it over the top, he just sat there and cried."

—MANNY AZENBERG,
Broadway producer

And so it was willed. A dream deferred for thousands of years. A dream hard-fought and won.

On May 14, 1948, the new government of the State of Israel, headed by David Ben-Gurion, was installed in Tel Aviv. For the first time since the Roman legions destroyed Jerusalem in the year 70 C.E., the Jewish people had a homeland of their own.

On March 17, 1969, Golda Meir, at seventy-one years of age, was nominated to be the third prime minister of Israel, a position she held until 1974, becoming the second female PM in the world. In a letter to her children after her death in 1978, Anwar al-Sadat wrote:

> I must record for history that she had been a noble foe during the phase of confrontation between us. . . . She had an undeniable role in starting this peace process. . . . She has always proved that she was a political leader of the first category, worthy of occupying her place in your history and worthy of the place she occupied in your leadership.

• • ● ● ● • •

AFTER ME . . .

This young man was among those who commanded an operation that was flawless. But to our deep sorrow this operation entailed a sacrifice of incomparable pain—the first among the storming party, the first to fall. . . . Of him . . . one may say in the words of David:

> They were swifter than eagles, they were stronger than lions . . .
>
> O Jonathan, thou wast slain in thine high places.
>
> I am distressed for thee, my brother Jonathan. . . .
>
> Thy love to me was wonderful.
>
> The same heroism in the man. The same lamentation in the heart of the people.
>
> —from the eulogy for
> Lieutenant Colonel Jonathan Netanyahu,
> Shimon Peres, July 6, 1976

On July 4, 1976, Lieutenant Colonel Jonathan Netanyahu, Israeli Defense Force, led a storming party that rescued 103 Jewish hostages from Entebbe Airport in Uganda, stunning the world and becoming a beacon against terrorism. When the rescue was virtually accomplished, Jonathan Netanyahu (Yoni) was shot to death by a Ugandan soldier. Yoni was the only member of the rescue force to die. This was in the high tradition of Israeli army officers, whose motto is "After me."

Yoni was thirty-years-old.

We Jews just refuse to disappear. No matter how strong . . . the forces against us . . . here we are. Millions of bodies broken, buried alive, burned to death, but never has anyone been able to succeed in breaking the spirit of the Jewish people.

—GOLDA MEIR

IN MY OWN LIFETIME

In my own lifetime, I want to see the fighting
   cease,

In my own lifetime, I want to enjoy the fruits
   of peace.

While I'm still here I want to know beyond a
   doubt that no one can lock us in or lock
   us out. . . .

In my own lifetime, I want to see our efforts
   blessed.

In my own lifetime, I want to see the walls
   come down and then I'll rest.

This Moses wants to see the Promised Land in
   my own lifetime!

—*The Rothschilds*,
the musical play, music by Jerry Bock, lyrics
by Sheldon Harnick

• • • ● • • •

A LITTLE OY

And if our good fortune never comes, here's to whatever comes . . .

A LITTLE JOY

How do we keep our balance? That I can tell you in a word—tradition!
                                        —Fiddler on the Roof

A new flood is predicted. Nothing can prevent it. In three days, the waters will wipe out the world.

The Dalai Lama appears on worldwide media and pleads with humanity to follow Buddhist teachings in order to find Nirvana in the wake of the disaster.

The Pope issues a similar message, saying, "It is still not too late to accept Jesus as your Savior."

The chief rabbi of Jerusalem takes a slightly different approach.

"My people," he says, "we have three days to learn how to live underwater."

Selected Sources

Over 250 sources were used. All were invaluable. The major ones are listed below.

BOOKS:

The Art of Jewish Cooking, Jennie Grossinger. Bantam, 1965.

Asimov Laughs Again, Isaac Asimov. HarperPerennial, 1992.

Avalon, Tin Men, and Diner: Three Screenplays by Barry Levinson. Atlantic Monthly Press, 1990.

The Big Book of Jewish Humor, William Novak and Moshe Waldoks. HarperPerennial, 1981.

A Bintel Brief, Volume II, Isaac Metzker. Viking, 1981.

The Book of Lists 90's Edition, David Wallechinsky and Irving Wallace. Little, Brown, 1993.

The Book of Lists 2, Irving Wallace. Bantam, 1980.

Broadway Anecdotes, Peter Hay. Oxford University Press, 1989.

By Any Other Name, Michael D. Shook. Prentice-Hall, 1994.

Call It Sleep, Henry Roth. Avon, 1965.

The Celebrity Almanac, Ed Lucaire. Prentice-Hall, 1991.

Complete Directory to Prime Time Network TV, Tim Brooks and Earle Marsh. Ballantine, 1988.

The Diary of a Young Girl, Anne Frank. Bantam, 1993.

A Dictionary of Yiddish Slang and Idioms, Fred Kogos. Citadel, 1998.

Entrepreneurs, Joseph J. and Suzy Fucini. G. K. Hall, 1985.

Fifth and Far Finer Than the First Four 637 Best Things Anybody Ever Said, Robert Byrne. Fawcett Crest, 1993.

The Filmgoers Book of Quotes, Leslie Halliwell. Hart-Davis, MacGibbon, 1973.

Funny People, Steve Allen. Stein and Day, 1981.

Getting Even, Woody Allen. Random House, 1975.

Great Jewish Quotations, Alfred J. Kolatch. Jonathan David, 1996.

Growing Up Jewish in America: An Oral History, Myrna Katz Frommer and Harvey Frommer. Harcourt Brace.

Guinness World Records 2000 Millennium Edition, Bantam, 2000.

Guinness World Records 2001. 2000.

How to Be a Jewish Mother, Dan Greenburg. Price Stern Sloan, 1979.

Illustrated Woody Allen Reader, Linda Sunshine. Knopf, 1993.

International Dictionary of 20th Century Biography. New American Library, 1987.

Isaac Asimov's Book of Facts, Isaac Asimov. Hastings House, 1992.

Leonard Maltin's 2000 Movie and Video Guide. Signet, 1999.

Jackie Mason's "The World According to Me!" Jackie Mason. Simon & Schuster, 1987.

Jackie Mason and Raoul Felder's Guide to New York City. Avon, 1997.

The Jewish Book of Lists, Joel Samberg. Citadel, 1999.

The Jewish Comedy Catalog, Darryl Lyman. Jonathan David, 1989.

The Jewish Connection, M. Hirsh Goldberg. Bantam, 1979.

The Jewish Festival Cook Book, Fannie Engle and Gertrude Blair. Warner, 1966.

Jewish Humor: What the Best Jewish Jokes Say About the Jews, Rabbi Joseph Telushkin. Morrow, 1998.

Jewish Proverbs, Brenda Rae Eno. Chronicle, 1989.

The Jewish Quiz Book, Dan Carlinsky. Doubleday, 1979.

The Joys of Yiddish, Leo Rosten. Pocket Books, 1970.

Meet the Folks, Sammy Levinson. Citadel, 1949.

Molly Goldberg Jewish Cook Book, Gertrude Berg and Myra Waldo. Pyramid, 1976.

More Funny People, Steve Allen. Stein and Day, 1982.

The Odd Index, Stephen Spignesi. Plume, 1994.

1001 Yiddish Proverbs, Fred Kogos. Citadel Press, 1997.

1911 Best Things Anybody Ever Said, Robert Byrne. Fawcett Columbine, 1988.

Our Crowd: The Great Jewish Families of the New York, Stephen Birmingham. Harper & Row, 1967.

People 1996 Entertainment Almanac, Cader Books, Little, Brown, 1995.

People's Almanac 2, David Wallechinsky and Irving Wallace. Morrow, 1978.

The People Weekly 1996 Entertainment Almanac. Little, Brown, 1996.

Pictorial History of the Jewish People, Nathan Ausubel. Crown, 1966.

The Portable Curmudgeon, Jon Winokur. New American Library, 1987.

Portnoy's Complaint, Philip Roth. Bantam, 1970.

The Quotable Einstein, Alice Calaprice. Princeton, 1997.

Roseanne, My Life as a Woman, Roseanne Barr. Harper & Row, 1989.

Schindler's List, Thomas Keneally. Touchstone, 1982.

Self Portrait of a Hero, Jonathan Netanyahu. Ballantine, 1980.

Sheila Levine Is Dead and Living in New York, Gail Parent. Bantam, 1973.

637 Best Things Anybody Ever Said No. 5, Robert Byrne. Ballantine, 1993.

Some Laughter, Some Tears, Sholom Aleichem. Putnam, 1969.

To Life! A Celebration of Jewish Being and Thinking, Rabbi Harold Kushner. Little, Brown, 1993.

A Treasury of Jewish Folklore, Nathan Ausubel. Crown, 1975.

The Ultimate Jewish Joke Book, Larry Wilde. Bantam, 1986.

Vagabond Stars, Nahma Sandrow. Seth Press, 1986.

We'll Always Have Paris, Robert A. Nowland and Gwendolyn W. Nolan. HarperCollins, 1995.

The Wise Men of Chelm, Samuel Tenenbaum. Collier, 1969.

Without Feathers, Woody Allen. Random House, 1975.

Yentl the Yeshiva Boy, Isaac Bashevis Singer. Farrar, Straus and Giroux, 1983.

Plays

Biloxi Blues, Neil Simon. Random House, 1986.

Brighton Beach Memoirs, Neil Simon. Random House, 1984

Broadway Bound, Neil Simon. Random House, 1987

Enter Laughing, Joseph Stein; adapted from the novel by Carl Reiner. Samuel French, 1964

Fiddler on the Roof, Joseph Stein. Pocket Books, 1971.

Lost in Yonkers, Neil Simon. Random House, 1991.

The Rothschilds, courtesy of MTI, 1970.

The Tenth Man, inspired by *The Dybbuk,* Paddy Chayefsky, 1959.

Films

Annie Hall, 1977

Television

A Laugh, A Tear, A Mitzvah, Roman Brygider, producer-director; Ron Rudaitis, producer; Sam Toperoff, writer; Roy Hammond, executive producer. Produced by WLIW21 Productions, Long Island, N.Y. ©1996 Heritage

INTERNET

Ahavat-Israel.com

Almondseed.com (Varian Fry Website)

BBC Online

Bergen.org/AAST/Projects/Yiddish/English/
    comwor

Bluep.com/~harryc/j-jokes2

Britannica.com

Ceemast.csupomona.edu/nova/yalow

Club.euronet.be/patrick.verboven/
    The-House-of-Lists/pseudonym

Collections of Unusual Facts: corsinet.com/
    trivia/1-triv

Cp-tel.net/miller/BilLee/quotes/Burns

Curtainup.com/sunshine

Dailynews.yahoo.com

Dorledor.org/advanvii-xii

Fallenmartyrs.com/sweden

The Forward.com/history

Geocities.com/Athens/Pantheon/1027/
    06db0223

German Information Center

Gildasclub.org

Globalicons.com/Legends/Burns/frame-career

Goldengate/08-History/Page1.html

Grasslot.com/s/halloffame

Harry's Black Hole

Haruth.com/JJ_personals.htm Hometown.aol.
   com/sillysongbook

Hickoksports.com/biograph/bernsnse.s

Infocom Online: infocom.com/~franklin/
   ininame/pmgl-001

Jewish-American Hall of Fame, All Rights
   Reserved (Jewish Museum in Cyberspace)

Jewishmusic.com/1568218958
   Muse.jhu.edu/demo/bhm/70.1br_ward

Jewishsports.com/reflections/koufax_yom

Jewishsports.net/baseball

Jewish Student Online Research Center: Jsource:
   Jewish Virtual Library www.us-israel.org/
   jsource/biography/wallenberg

Jewish Telegraph: www.tcom.co.uk/hpnet/jt3

Jewish War Veterans of the USA: Jtsa.edu/users/
   hsp/htm/mbrooks

Judaica Collections of Florida Atlantic University,
   FAU Wimberly Library Special Collections

Lib.ou.edu/depts/bass/seligman (Bizzell
   Memorial Library, University of Oklahoma at
   Norman)

Links in Chassidic Legacy

Mit.edu/invent/www/inventorsR-Z/strauss

Members.aol.com/RSVNorton/Lincoln14.html

Nando.net/ Scripps Howard: Interview by Wayne
    Bledsoe, April 4, 1998, *Knoxville
    News-Sentinel*

Naomi's Collection of Jewish Humor: drapkin.
    demon.co.uk/jh

NYTimes.com

Nycatskills.com

Northwestern.edu/~pomeroi/Humor/tashlich.htm

Pasadena.wr.usgs.gov/cahist_eqs

Peterpaulandmary.com

Quotations.about.com/arts/quotations/library/
    db/bltop_proverb_yid

Whoosh!www.whoosh.org/issue34/error3.html

us-israel.org/jsource/biography/Resnik.html:
    Judith Resnik: By Seymour "Sy" Brody

U.S. Geological Survey, California Earthquake
    History

University of MichiganWell.com/user/argv/
    funny/jewish-names

Windows.umich.edu/cgi-bin/tour_def/people/
    astronauts/wolf.

Windows.umich.edu/people/enlightenment/
    herschel

Zbach.com/page 17/jewishads

INTERVIEWS

Bernie Allen
Marty Allen
Broadway's Jerusalem 2
Arthur C. Clarke
Pat Cooper
Sandy Hackett
Jay Leno staff
B. Manischewitz Company
Moment Magazine
Michael McDonough, MTI
Oklahoma Historical Society
Pudgy! The Queen of Tease
Freddie Roman
Professor Tony Rothman
Levi Strauss & Co., San Francisco
Stan Zimmerman
Congregation Shearith Israel, NYC
Temple Emanu-El, NYC